PHRENOLOGY

BY

CHARLES H. OLIN

AUTHOR OF "VENTRILOQUISM," "SOCIALISM," &c.

HOW TO TELL YOUR OWN
AND YOUR FRIENDS' CHAR-
ACTER AND FORTUNE BY
THE SHAPE OF THE HEAD

PHILADELPHIA
THE PENN PUBLISHING COMPANY
1923

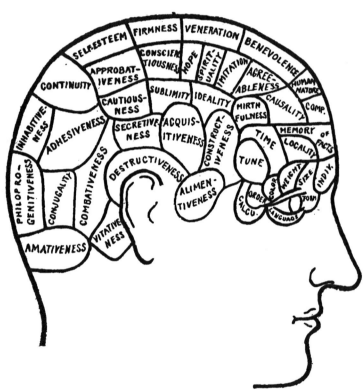

FIG. 1. The organs and their locations

Contents

CONTENTS

CONTENTS

PHRENOLOGY

INTRODUCTION

THE PHRENOLOGIST AND THE SKEPTIC

SEVERAL years ago, at South Deerfield, Massachusetts, a certain Nelson Sizer and a Dr. Buell were giving lectures on Phrenology. Two or three had already been given, and the whole people seemed aroused on the subject.

Not all, however, were believers. The enthusiasm and apparent sincerity of the lecturers had made a favorable impressson on many, but there were some who, like the people of Missouri, wanted to be " shown " in order to believe.

Others were frankly skeptical of the phrenologists' claims. The foremost of these was a certain Dr. A——. The idea that any one, no matter how sincere or honest he might appear to be, could actually read the character of an individual from the shape and appearance of his head—nay, more, could even tell what a person's disposition had

7

been during life by an examination of his skull
after death—to this practical man seemed absurd.

True, during his previous lectures, Professor
Sizer, by examining the heads of well-known persons in the audience, had made some striking and
truthful statements; but still the good Doctor believed that it must be all " bosh." So he decided
to set a trap for the phrenologist; he would
"stump" him for once and laugh him and his pre-
tended science out of town. Doubtless, as he pre-
pared for the Professor's downfall, he chuckled
gleefully to himself, and thought of the moment
of triumph that would be his.

At any rate, when the phrenologist was about to
begin his lecture one evening, Dr. A—— immediately rose and asked permission to say that he had a
skull with him which he desired to submit for public examination at the close of the lecture. " I
knew the person well to whom the skull belonged," he said, "and have written the facts so as
to compare them with your statement when you
are done."

"Very well," was the answer. " But we will
not wait until the close of the lecture, for if we
make a mistake, as the Doctor evidently hopes and
expects we will, the audience may not care to hear

anything more on the subject, and I may not feel
in the mood to lecture. So, if we are to be van-
quished, I prefer to have it done while I am in full
strength. Please bring forward the skull."

This was done, and while the audience remained
in an excited whispering state the two phrenologists carefully examined the ghastly object. By
putting a lighted candle in it behind their desk,
they found that the bone was thin enough in some
places to allow the light to shine through. This
was especially true at the sides and back, which in
former lectures they had declared to be the region
of the passions and animal instincts. But in front,
where they had declared the intellect had its seat
in the living brain, all was dark, showing that the
bone was very thick, except on each side. There,
just where they had taught the organ of Tune was
located, on a space about as large as a quarter of a
dollar, the light was very bright, and the bone
seemed scarcely thicker than letter-paper. Be-
sides, the front half of the skull seemed heavy, so
much so that when held in the centre it balanced
forward with a bump. The form of the head was
like that of a female, the general quality of the
bone delicate, and the teeth young.

Finally, Dr. Sizer turned to the audience and

called for some one to take down all that might be said, for comparison with the Doctor's paper. All things being ready, and the crowd painfully intent to hear every word, Professor Sizer said:

"This is the skull of a female about twenty years old. She had a well-balanced head and character, up to about fourteen years of age; was bright and intelligent, a good scholar, and ambitious, energetic and affectionate; but something happened about that time that spoiled her intellect, with the single exception that her musical talent remained very active. Meanwhile, the propensities were made unduly active; and not being regulated by the intellect or moral sentiments, she became quarrelsome, cruel, cunning, avaricious, gluttonous, and inclined to social debasement."

He then called upon the Doctor to send up his paper giving the person's history.

The Doctor hesitated. "I am willing to admit," he said, reluctantly, "that your description in some respects corresponds with the real character, but of course it is all guesswork."

"Doctor," replied Professor Sizer, "you brought this skull and offered it as a challenge, saying you had the sketch written in your pocket; that you knew all about the person who carried the skull, and now you try to palm off an oral statement and insult us by the claim that if we have in any sense described the person, it is 'guesswork.' This course is unfair, it is unmanly, and being a medical man, it is wholly unprofessional. I demand 'Cæsar's will,' and hope the gentlemen near the door will not permit the Doctor to carry it away. It is due to the audience, it is due to us, it is due to the Doctor, and to truth, that we have it to compare with our statement."

At this the audience set up such a clamor that the medical man was forced to comply. The statement was sent up and read by a prominent deacon in the hall, amid a silence that could be felt. It ran as follows :

"The skull presented is that of a girl who was remarkably bright in every respect, and possessed a most excellent disposition until she was about fourteen and a half years old. She was forward as a scholar, and excellent in music. She took a heavy cold, followed by brain fever, and when she recovered from it her intellect was utterly gone except the single faculty of music, and though she lived six years as an idiot, she would sing like a nightingale. Her temper became very violent, and she was a terror to her friends, and what was worse, she became vulgar and obscene. She was a patient of mine, and I knew her entire history."

The audience listened to the reading of this statement, and then broke out in prolonged applause. Even Dr. A—— was convinced. Going forward, he grasped the phrenologist's hand, saying: "This removes the only stumbling-block I had in regard to the acceptance of Phrenology. I thought a head so well shaped would deceive you ; but you have not only described her as she really was before she was ill, but as she was after sickness spoiled her, which I thought it impossible for anybody to do."

This striking incident, and many others like it to be found in the history of the subject, proves that Phrenology is a real science, as its teachers claim, and not a mere branch of so-called fortune-telling.

The difference between the phrenologist and the ordinary fortune-teller is this. The reader of cards or the like, and the seer of visions, gets, or pretends to get, his knowledge by other than natural means. This the expert phrenologist never does. He will, however, read you as an open book, and show a surprising knowledge of your weak and strong points. But he will not pretend to be able to tell the history of your life from the cradle to the grave—whether you are happy or unhappy, rich or poor, married or single, or if you have a long or short life before you. True, he may draw wise conclusions respecting those things, but these are based wholly upon his expert knowledge of the various characteristics revealed to him, not by visions or outside aid of any kind, but by the human head alone. He will tell you accurately what you are best fitted for, and in what direction you can be successful, if you will make the most of your natural talents and strive to lessen by proper mental exercise and control, the bad qualities in you which he sees. True, there are some so-called phrenologists who throw an air of mystery around their readings. Their signs may be seen swinging from the windows of cheap lodging-houses in every large city, but they really have very little knowledge of Phrenology. It is largely because the general public does not know the difference between the real and the false that the subject is not better understood and more popular at the present time.

PHRENOLOGY AS A SCIENCE

Phrenology is a true science, the principles of

which may be learned and applied if sufficient time and attention are given to the study. The word itself comes from the Greek—" phren," meaning mind, and " logos," science. It is, in fact, the science of the mind.

Mind itself is, of course, something that cannot be seen. We all know that it exists because we are able to think and reason, but just what it is, no one seems to feel exactly sure. This much, however, can be said of it: it requires a material organ to work through ; that organ is the brain. It is by the brain that the phrenologist is able to read character. He makes no attempt to define the nature of the mind, but simply asserts that the brain is the physical instrument by and through which it acts.

This is evident because where there is no brain there is no intelligence or power to think, as in the case of idiots whose heads, and therefore brains, are small and undeveloped when compared with the heads of men noted for their ability to think and reason. Serious injuries to the head often affect the mind, while similar injuries to other parts of the body leave it unharmed. So, too, disease in the brain may produce loss of memory and intelligence, or bring about insanity, while mechanical pressure thereon often destroys all mental power.

Therefore, the phrenologist rightly studies the brain of an individual for evidence of his mental strength and natural traits. As these together form the character of a person, a knowledge of what they are show his weak and strong points, and account for his success or failure in the various lines of human effort.

Although it is not to be expected that every one can become as expert as Nelson Sizer[1] was in this line, as he was unusually gifted and had the advantage of nearly fifty years' experience as a phrenologist, there is no reason why great skill and accuracy may not be acquired by all who are willing to give the necessary time and application to a thorough study of the subject.

[1] Professor Sizer was for forty-six years chief phrenological examiner in the office of Fowler & Wells, who devoted their lives to spreading the truths of this science ; president of the American Institute of Phrenology ; author of "Forty Years in Phrenology," "How to Study Strangers," and many other valuable works on the subject. During his lifetime he examined the heads of more than 250,000 persons, and spent fifty-six years in lecturing on human character in all parts of the United States. His experience with the skeptic, given in the foregoing pages, was adapted from "Forty Years in Phrenology," as copied from his original diary.

In the following pages are set forth the teachings of the great phrenologists of the past, together with the latest and best ideas on the subject, in what is intended to be a simple, clear and interesting manner. So much has been written, and well written, about Phrenology that the author makes no claim to anything new or original. But while his task has been one mainly of selection from the works of Combe, Wells, Sizer, Hyde, and others, he has aimed to present the complete principles of the science in language which all can readily understand, and in a popular and instructive way.

CHAPTER I

THE VALUE AND IMPORTANCE OF PHRENOLOGY

"THE principal study of mankind," wrote Alexander Pope, "is man." In this saying was compressed not only the results of the poet's own observation and experience, but the wisdom of the ages.

Nor is it less true in our day than it was in his. In the whole field of human inquiry there is nothing more important or more interesting than a knowledge of human character, for only by knowing that can a man fully know himself.

Yet, strangely enough, the study of man has not received the attention it deserves at the hands of those who aspire to be teachers of men. True, the warmth of the poet's imagination and the accuracy of observation belonging to the historian and the novelist have given to the world glowing descriptions of the passions, desires, longings, ambitions, and all the various feelings which control the hidden springs of human action. But these

17

pictures, though vivid, lack the agreement and clear-cut analysis which should form the basis of any real science of character.

Nearly all of us, however, are in some degree character readers—or think we are. Almost unconsciously we judge men by the impression they make upon us by their gait, the manner in which they carry themselves and wear their clothes, the quality of their dress and mode of speech. All of these are significant outward signs of certain inward impulses. Yet in themselves they fall short of forming a complete index of the real mental and spiritual traits of man.

We may indeed form an opinion of a person based on a single observation. That opinion is usually formed in great part by the impression conveyed to us by the person's face; in other words, we are, to some extent at least, physiognomists.

PHYSIOGNOMY

Like other sciences, physiognomy is a system of character reading, developed slowly by observation through the long experience of years. It has been made possible by the knowledge that men express their feelings, passions, and thoughts in their faces and bodily attitudes. But, unfortunately for the practical use of the science, the expression of the face may be changed at will, and by constant attention and practice the features may be set into an entirely misleading expression. A sharper or a thief may thus hide his real nature and purposes behind a look of honesty and good will.

PRACTICAL BASIS OF PHRENOLOGY

But this is not true of the skull, the size and shape of which cannot be changed at will by its owner. Therefore, Phrenology, because it has discovered and proved that the size, form, and appearance of the head correspond with the traits and inclinations of the individual, is of the utmost practical importance. By its aid we are able to gauge our own capacity, to know our strong and weak points, and to learn what vices most easily beset us. Forewarned is forearmed, and knowing ourselves as we are, we can set about the work of self-improvement intelligently, and with the best prospects of complete success.

Next in importance to self-knowledge is a knowledge of our fellows. Especially is this true of those with whom we are brought into close relations, either at home or in daily and hourly contact in the business world. Upon our knowledge of the defects and virtues of others with whom we are associated depends much of our happiness and well being. Anything that helps us to read character as one reads a printed page, is consequently to be welcomed as an aid to our own progress in life. The principles of Phrenology, if carefully studied and applied, will enable us largely to attain this end.

It also becomes of great use in the measures taken to reform criminals, and even in aiding the mildly insane. Without the sure knowledge that Phrenology gives, reformers and educators are working more or less in the dark; by the flood of light which it throws upon human character they are able to work with nature and not against it, toward the desired end.

If, for example, a person is found with any special organ unusually developed—say Destructiveness, which, when too large, gives the desire to kill—all the circumstances which are liable to excite that organ should be removed, while those organs which restrain the promptings of Destructiveness should be made more active. So with all the organs ; the activity of those that tend toward evil should be lessened, while those that have an influence for good should be strengthened. Where a natural talent for anything is shown to exist— say for music or art—the individual should be encouraged to still further develop it by such study and practice as will tend to make it stronger.

ITS USE AND MISSION

Phrenology is also of great use in choosing men for positions of trust. Take two men, for instance, who seem to have about the same amount of ability and experience for an important office requiring honesty and virtue. But suppose that one has a strongly-developed, well-rounded top-head, while the lower part of the head in the other is larger and his crown nearly flat. The practical phrenologist would at once choose the man with the high top-head and less strong lower head, because a high crown shows excellent moral qualities.

Even as a source of pleasure and amusement this science gives to the student the power to gratify the curiosity of his friends and arouse their amazement; but that, of course, is its smallest value. Its true mission is to bring about a proper growth and harmony of all those powers which make a man useful and respected in his home life, among his friends, and in the world at large.

FOUNDED ON NATURAL LAWS

Nor is Phrenology a matter of vague and uncertain theories. Its principles have been proved to be sound and correct too many times in the past to be disputed by any except those who are blind to the value of facts and the weight of human testimony. No mere pretender assisted at its birth; it was founded on no vain dream of the imagination; it was based on laws of human nature as sound and true as the laws of any great science. In the street and the crowded lecture hall, in schools and colleges, in prisons and insane asylums, in churches and theatres, and among the savage tribes and civilized peoples of the world it has been tried and not found wanting.

HISTORY—DR. GALL

Phrenology was first discovered and applied to character delineation by Dr. Franz Joseph Gall, a German physician, born in 1758. As a boy given to observation, he was struck by the diversity of talent and disposition among his companions at play or in the schoolroom. Some excelled in penmanship, others in arithmetic; some acquired a knowledge of languages with little effort, while some learned by heart anything they desired with the greatest ease.

Both at school and later when he entered a university, he noticed that those who surpassed him in the ability to repeat by rote, all had prominent eyes. This led him to believe that there was an important connection between the two. After much reflection he concluded that, if memory for words was indicated by an external sign, such might be the case with the other intellectual powers. Continuing his observations, he at last became convinced that strongly marked traits of character and degrees of talent were associated with corresponding peculiarities in the form of the head.

His interest now thoroughly aroused, he devoted more than twenty years to study and observation along this special line. Not only did he make collections of skulls and casts of heads of persons noted for special mental attainments, but he visited prisons, schools and colleges, studying and comparing the development of the crania of thousands of persons. Thus by slow and painstaking methods he found external signs which indicated a decided disposition for painting, music, and the mechanical arts. Later he discovered the signs of the moral sentiments.

But it is to be noted that in making these observations Dr. Gall never for a moment thought that the shape of the skull accounted for the different talents, as those ignorant of the subject have sometimes represented. From the first, he referred the influence, whatever it was, to the brain. This he taught was merely the organ of the mind, which shaped the skull and which expressed the individuality or soul of its possessor. Thus the actual cause was traced back to its proper source. He taught also that different parts of the brain are connected with different functions of the body ; and that, other things being equal, size of the brain and its various parts is an indication of mental power.

J. G. SPURZHEIM

Beginning his lectures on his system at Vienna in 1796, he continued the work there for five years, with the assistance of Dr. J. G. Spurzheim, a convert to Phrenology, who not only added many valuable discoveries to those of his master regarding the structure and operations of the brain, but contributed much to shape the fruits of their united labors into a beautiful and logical system of mental philosophy. Together they lectured in the chief cities of Northern Europe, and finally settled in Paris in 1807.

COMBE

During a visit to England in 1813, Spurzheim became acquainted with George Combe, a man of great mental power and an ardent seeker of the truth ; but also very cautious in accepting anything new and untried.

At first Combe regarded the new science with doubt and unbelief, but was so impressed by Dr. Spurzheim's method in showing the detailed structure of the human brain by dissection, that his interest and admiration were aroused.

Careful observation and comparison of the variations in the form of the skulls of men of known mental traits or talents, convinced Combe that these variations corresponded to the differ- ence in their recognized qualities. He found, in other words, that their individual traits agreed with the growth of the corresponding organs o the brain as set forth by Gall and Spurzheim. For the rest of his life he was a strong teacher of the new theory, and gave many striking demonstrations of its accuracy.

To these three men the world is indebted for its knowledge of Phrenology. In many European countries, as well as in the United States, which he visited, Combe was welcomed in the best social, scientific and political circles as a brilliant religious, social and educational reformer and deep thinker. Both he and Dr. Gall were men of exceptional intelligence, careful observers, close reasoners, and prone to arrive at conclusions only on overwhelming evidence.

To suppose that their work is founded on error is unjust and untrue. All their discoveries in anatomy and physiology, which were bitterly opposed at the time, are now admitted by the lead ers in these lines to be sound and true. Phrenologists are not afraid of their science; they have begged and even demanded investigation. The heads of thousands of persons unknown to them have been successfully read, and it is significant that those who have laughed at the claims of Phrenology and misquoted its teachings and principles have never succeeded in disproving it. And it is a fact strongly in favor of the science that those who have made a thorough study of its princi-

ples according to the natural rules laid down by phrenologists, have ended by believing in the science.[1]

TESTIMONY OF A GREAT ENGLISH SCHOLAR

Even among the scholars of to-day Phrenology
is not without its staunch defenders. In his book,
"The Wonderful Century," published in 1889,
Alfred Russell Wallace, the well-known English
naturalist and author, names Phrenology—" a
science," he says, " of whose substantial truth and
vast importance I have no more doubt than I
have of the value and importance of any of the
great intellectual advances already recorded "—as
the chief of the important lines of investigation
affecting our own intellectual and spiritual nature
which has been neglected. It was, he declares,
" founded step by step on observation and comparison of facts, confirmed and checked in every
conceivable way, and subjected to the most rigid
tests. . . . Three men of exceptional talents
and acuteness of observation devoted their lives
to the collection of these facts. And it was only
after making allowance for every source of uncertainty or error that they announced the possi-

[1] Thomas A. Hyde, in "The True Basis for the Science of
Mind."

bility of determining character with a considerable amount of certainty, and often with marvelous exactness. Surely this was a scientific mode of procedure, and the only sound method of ascertaining the relations that exist between the development of the brain and the mental faculties and powers. . . . To reject such determinations without full examination of the evidence in support of them, without applying any of the careful tests which the early phrenologists applied, and on the mere vague allegations of insufficient observation or unscientific method, is itself truly unscientific."

His Prediction

In concluding his very interesting consideration of the whole subject, Professor Wallace asserts that in the present century Phrenology will surely attain general acceptance. It will, he says, prove itself to be the true science of the mind ; and its persistent neglect and obloquy during the last sixty years will then be referred to as an example of the almost incredible narrowness and prejudice which prevailed among men of science at the very time they were making such splendid advances in other fields of thought and discovery.

CHAPTER II

BRAIN AND SKULL

House of the Brain

THE size, form, and development of the brain are shown by the skull, the outer surface of which gives with sufficient accuracy an idea of the surface of the brain itself. In other words, the brain forms the skull in its own likeness and completely fills it from the opening of the eyes to the back of the neck, even as the soft mass of an egg fills the shell. The skull is simply the house the brain lives in; but it is made to protect it and not to confine it.

In an unborn child the brain is formed before the skull that covers it, and the whole is so made that during youth and early manhood it readily accommodates itself to the growing mental organs within.

Bone is Living Matter

In spite of its apparent hardness all bone is living matter, receiving nourishment and building materials from the blood, just as the muscles do.

When the brain needs more room in one particular part—because that part is excited or exercised more than other parts—the bone wears thinner there, its material being dissolved and carried into the general circulation ; while new bony matter is formed on the outside a little further on, thus causing the skull to increase in size at such points. When the activity of the mind—which works not through the brain as a whole, but through various portions or organs in it—is the same in all parts of the brain, the growth of the skull is regular over its entire surface.

Skull in Old Age

In old age, where the brain remains active, the skull sometimes becomes very thin, because the bone-making elements in the blood are only sufficient to form the bone slowly, and some of the substance of the skull is taken up to keep the working bones of the human frame in proper condition. Where the brain is not active, and shrinks from lack of use, just as a muscle grows weak and flabby from want of exercise, while yet there is enough bone-making material in the food, the skull thickens to fill the space caused by the dwindling brain.

Now Phrenology teaches that known differences of character correspond to certain differences in the size, shape, and general condition of the skull.

FORM SHOWS CHARACTER

For example, men who have become famous as thinkers and reasoners have large heads and high, broad foreheads. Men with little or no reasoning power have small flat heads with slanting foreheads. The skulls of men in whom the animal instincts prevail are largely developed at the back, while those who are very religious or moral have a large top-head. So also the exercise of any faculty or talent leaves its sign upon the skull, which can be read by the expert phrenologist almost as plainly as the sign of a shopkeeper above his door. Thus the true nature of the man under examination is revealed to him.

PHRENOLOGY NOT BUMPOLOGY

The popular idea that Phrenology is bumpology —that is, that it is based on bumps and hollow places in the human head—is a mistaken one. If that were all there is to Phrenology, the phrenologist would fail when confronted by a man with a head as smooth as a billiard ball.   Yet such persons often prove to be most excellent subjects for phrenological study.   The skull of the average man does not look like the waves of the sea, the crest showing power and the trough weakness.

MEASUREMENTS

Measurements from the opening of the ear, be

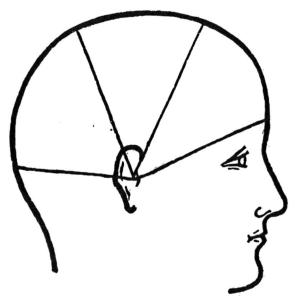

FIG. 2.

hind which is located the centre of the brain, to the surface of the head in various direction, really tell the story. (See Fig. 2.) Two heads may be

found of the same length from the forehead to the
back-head; but one will be two inches wider above
and about the ears than the other. They may
also be of the same height from the ear upward,
the difference showing in the growth of the side-
head—the head in one case being broad and in the
other narrow.

VARIATIONS IN FORM

One head may have a forehead that sticks out
in the lower part, but slants upward and backward; another may show a moderate development
across the brows and a heavy upper forehead,
forming what is often called a beetling forehead.
Another is narrow at the temples, but wide and
massive below. One head may be heavy just
above the ears and taper both ways, front and
rear; another seems wide in the upper back region
and high and narrow in front. One is straight
up and down at the back, while a second stands
out in a long, graceful curve. Still another is
high at the crown; one is well rounded in the
middle and top-head, while some are flat in that
region. In others there seems to be a kind of
hollow at the top—that is, it is less than flat
there.

Knowing the mental faculties which are situated behind these different places, the phrenologist is able to judge of their development merely by the form of the head alone.

RACIAL DIFFERENCES

The skulls of races and peoples differ widely in form and size. The average member of the white race has a high and bulging forehead and crown and a moderately developed back-head, as compared with other races. The skull of the North American Indian, on the contrary, is noticeable for its roundness; it has great breadth immediately above the ears and a rather high crown. The forehead, although broad in its lower part, is not high, and runs backward toward the top-head. If a slanting line were drawn from just under the tip of the nose to the middle of the crown, a good portion of the forehead in the white race would be found outside or overlapping the line, while most of the forehead of the Indian or the uneducated Negro would appear inside.

The skull, or cranium, of the Negro is usually long and narrow from front to back, presenting a striking difference when compared with that of his white brother.

Likewise there are marked differences in the skulls of the various nations, each having its own special type.

MALE AND FEMALE SKULLS

The heads of men and women differ in shape almost as much as do their bodily forms. The cranium of a man rises higher from the opening of the ear to the top of the back-head, and is more largely developed in its lower back part than is the skull of his sister. In her case the bones are less heavy and strong; they are smoother and more delicate. The head is also not so thick at its base, nor so high at the top of the upper back-head. The crown, however, is usually more rounded. These differences, as will be shown later when we come to take up the location of the various organs, correspond to the natural habits and duties of the two sexes.

CHAPTER III

THE BASIS OF PHRENOLOGY

Importance of Observation

THE first thing necessary to establish a science of character is observation. So widely do men differ from each other in character and mental ability that it is impossible to build up a science like Phrenology by reflection alone. When the seat of an organ and its function are known, we can infer the presence of either in the absence of the other, as observation has taught us they are related. For example, largely developed lungs in an animal, other things, such as health, being equal, show great breathing power; so also when the stomach is present we may confidently assert that the powers of digestion will be manifested. Should both of these organs be absent, we can declare that breathing and digestion, at least according to ordinary processes, will not be manifest.

In like manner, the phrenologist, having found in the brain the physical seat of the various powers of the human mind, is able to set forth the functions of each.

PHRENOLOGY AND ANIMALS

Thus, if it has been ascertained that the disposition to fight or defend oneself is connected with a physical organ for its manifestation, then the presence of that organ indicates that the instinct of defense will form an element in the character of those possessing that organ. In those animals which are aggressive in the assertion of their rights, as, for instance, the cock, Phrenology has shown that the organ corresponding to Combativeness in the human brain is largely developed; while in those animals which are of a timid nature and have little disposition to resist attack, as in the case of sheep, it is deficient. So also the beaver, which is noted for its building ability, has a large organ of Constructiveness. The squirrel, which in a wild state spends most of its days in laying up food for the winter, has a large organ of Acquisitiveness. On the other hand, many animals that do not construct houses or make provision for the future, have a weak development of these organs.

Once the seat of a faculty has been found by

observation, as when Dr. Gall observed that large eyes invariably indicated a talent for language, many opportunities are open for watching its manifestations, for these can be readily noted from time to time, and their degrees of power and activity measured. The existence of an organ which long continued notice has shown to be invariably largely developed in persons showing a certain pronounced tendency, thus implies the existence of that tendency.

It is of course understood that the relations between the various faculties and the different folds of the brain had always existed, but up to the time of Dr. Gall, they had never been determined. That has been the case with many great discoveries, the truth of which the world now acknowledges.

The revolution of the planets had doubtless continued since they were created; the laws which regulate the planetary systems have ever operated as at present; and the blood in the human body has circulated in the same way since man was made. Yet it was not until Copernicus, Newton, and Harvey, respectively, first revealed the great laws of the universe and of their own being that men knew the mystery of their operation.

So with Phrenology. Upon the development, shape and quality of the brain the mind has always relied. Yet no man could understand, much less explain this, until Dr. Gall and his colaborers became the instruments to discover and present this important truth.

MIND A COLLECTION OF FACULTIES

It has been denied by some that the mind acts through a combination of faculties seated in different portions of the brain; but as every one knows, the mind is made up of many separate faculties or powers as shown by its varied operations. It is natural to infer, therefore, that the brain has a corresponding separate organ for each faculty. That such is the case is proved by evidence which cannot be lightly set aside or successfully disputed.

This is strictly in accordance with the law operating in all other parts of the human system— throughout all nature, in fact. As the eye and the ear have separate duties, and can never perform the duties of each other, so the different folds of the brain have their separate duties to which each is limited. Thus, one fold is the organ of Benevolence, another the organ of Firmness.

If the mind were a single faculty or unit, then the man who could do one thing well, could do anything else equally well, which we know is not so. One man can write good poetry, but is perhaps unable to sing well. Another is a good mechanic, but a poor reasoner; a third reasons well, but cannot excel in figures.

MENTAL POWER DEPENDS ON BRAIN DEVELOPMENT

When we learn that there are as many organs of the brain as faculties of the mind, we see that some of these organs may be large, while others are small. If, therefore, one organ or set of organs is well developed, then the faculties which depend upon it are active and strong. If Time and Tune be large, there will be the power to sing; or if Constructiveness, Imitation, Size, Weight, etc., be large, the person may be a good mechanic, but a poor scholar or a bad reasoner.

ORGANS DETERMINED BY COMPARISON

Phrenology does not pretend that the functions of the various windings of the brain can be ascertained by anatomy or physiology. It would be as difficult to decide this matter by inspection, as to decide upon the use of any particular nerve when separated from the human system. The nerves of emotion and sensation, though similar in appearance, perform very different offices. It is the same with those bundles of nerves which make up the folds of the brain. The only way to decide upon the office of any part of the brain is by observing a similar trait of character in various persons, and then finding wherein the heads of these persons are alike.

Proofs

In this way, and in this way alone, Dr. Gall was enabled to find the different organs. The accuracy with which he mapped out their seats in the human brain is shown by the effects which injuries upon the skull have produced. In one case where a part of the skull was broken so as to press upon the brain, the organ which was pressed lost its power, but on removing the cause this power returned. When, at another time, the skull was removed over the organ of Firmness, pressure upon that part of the brain destroyed the balance of mind. In another case the organs of Language and Individuality were exposed, with the result that when the finger was placed upon them the patient could not call by name her most intimate friends. But on removing the finger her memory returned.

Phreno-Magnetism

Hypnotism also furnishes striking evidence of the truth of Phrenology, as will be seen by the following quotation from an article by Dr. George F. Laidlaw in a recent number of the "Metropolitan Magazine."

"There is one curious phenomenon in hypnotism," writes Dr. Laidlaw, " which I have never been able to explain satisfactorily, and which seems to be ignored by the modern hypnotist. It was first studied by Braid. It is called phreno-magnetism and has been advanced by the phrenologists in proof of the correctness of their localization of the mental faculties on the head. So far as I know it has never received serious consideration from scientists, perhaps because based on two theories that modern science has not yet accepted; first, that there is such a thing as animal magnetism and, secondly, that the phrenologists have correctly located the faculties of the human head. However this may be, phreno-magnetism is a phenomenon which can be tested readily by any one interested. The technic of phreno-magnetism is this : When the subject is in the hypnotic sleep, the operator, standing behind him, places the tips of his fingers upon the subject's head and waits. Soon the subject will begin to act or sing or speak. Any one acquainted with the phrenological system of localization will recognize at once that the actions or words of the subject correspond to the ' organ ' on the head which has been touched by the operator. Thus, if you touch Combativeness the subject is very apt to square off and strike some one or speak of war or a drum. If you touch Veneration, he is very apt to lift his eyes and pray. I have heard a very eloquent sermon thus inspired in a subject who was gifted with a ready tongue. Touch the organ of Color and he will speak of beautiful colors. Touch Tune and he will sing or whistle. Touch Caution and his face will express vivid fear. I remember that one subject startled me by shouting, ' Look out ! ' and making a leap that he could scarcely have equaled in his waking state. When I touched the faculty of Caution, he thought he saw a snake."

CHAPTER IV

DEFINITION OF THE ORGANS

DR. GALL succeeded in locating twenty-six of the organs of the brain, and others were discovered by Spurzheim, Combe, Caldwell, the Fowlers and other noted phrenologists. Each succeeding investigator availed himself of all that had been proved true and useful, and added thereto his own observations and experience. The usually accepted number is now forty-two, defined as follows:

1. *Amativeness.* Love between the sexes—Desire to marry.
2. *Conjugality.* Matrimony—Love of one—Union for life.
3. *Philoprogenitiveness.* Parental love—Regard for offspring—Fondness for pets.
4. *Adhesiveness.* Friendship — Sociability—Love of society.
5. *Inhabitiveness.* Love of home and country.
6. *Continuity, or Concentrativeness.* One thing at a time—Consecutiveness.

7. *Vitativeness.* Love and tenacity of life—Dread of Annihilation.

8. *Combativeness.* Resistance — Defense — Courage—Opposition.

9. *Destructiveness.* Inclination to destroy—Force—Anger—Severity.

10. *Alimentiveness.* Appetite — Hunger — Love of food, drink, etc.

11. *Acquisitiveness.* Love of wealth and possessions—Frugality—Economy.

12. *Secretiveness.* Disposition to conceal; to work in secret; to disguise one's feelings—Reserve—Discretion.

13. *Cautiousness.* Prudence—Watchfulness—Care.

14. *Approbativeness.* Love of praise—Desire to please—Desire for popular applause or fame—Ambition.

15. *Self-esteem.* Self-respect—Independence—Self-confidence—Dignity—Pride.

16. *Firmness.* Decision of character—Perseverance—Stability—Strength of will.

17. *Conscientiousness.* Love of right—Sense of justice—Integrity—Conscience.

18. *Hope.* Optimism—Pleasant anticipation—Enterprise.

19. *Spirituality.* Faith—Intuition—Belief in God.

20. *Veneration.* Reverence for sacred things —Devotion—Respect for superiors in rank and power.

21. *Benevolence.* Kindness—Goodness—Sympathy—Compassion—Generosity.

22. *Constructiveness.* Talent for making, contriving and building—Mechanical ingenuity.

23. *Ideality.* Refinement—Love of beauty— Taste—Purity.

24. *Sublimity.* Delight in grand thoughts or scenes—Love of grandeur.

25. *Imitation.* Ability to copy, describe, to follow models, to imitate.

26. *Mirthfulness.* Sense of humor—Natural wit—Love of fun—Perception of the absurd.

27. *Individuality.* Power of observation— Desire to see and examine.

28. *Form.* Recollection of shape—Memory of persons and faces.

29. *Size.* Ability to measure by the eye and give judgment of the distance, height, weight, dimensions, etc.

30. *Weight.* Judgment of the resistance of bodies—Firmness on the feet in balancing and climbing, etc.—Perception of the law of Gravity.

31. *Color.* Love of and ability to judge colors and distinguish their different shades.

32. *Order.* Love of system—Method—Neatness—Arrangement.

33. *Numbers, or Calculation.* Talent for numbers and mental arithmetic.

34. *Locality.* Recollection of roads, places, and scenery. Memory of the relative position of bodies—Liking for Geography.

35. *Eventuality.* Memory of facts and circumstances.

36. *Time.* Ability to measure the duration and succession of time—Punctuality.

37. *Tune.* Sense of harmony and melody—Love of music—Ability to learn and remember tunes.

38. *Language.* Memory of words or arbitrary signs—Ready expression of ideas.

39. *Causality.* Disposition to search out the cause of every effect—Love of investigation—Originality.

40. *Comparison.* Ability to acquire and judge of the quality of different things—Ability to analyze and illustrate.

41. *Human Nature.* Perception of character and motives.

42. *Agreeableness.* Pleasantness—Amiability—Persuasiveness.

THE GROUPING OF THE ORGANS

That perfect adaptation of means. to an end, which marks all the works of God, is beautifully illustrated by the arrangement of the various organs of the brain in groups. As in the body, as a whole, the seat of every mental power in man is just that which best fits it for its special duty, and grouped around it, for its support and active co-operation, are those organs which come into close relationship with it.

LOBES OF THE BRAIN

As a whole, the brain is divided, to the right and left, into halves, or hemispheres, by a membrane called the falciform, which, hanging down from the arch of the skull, runs from the middle line of the forehead to the back part of the head. On each side of the dividing line between these halves, the same organ occurs. All the organs are therefore double, in the same manner as are the eyes, the ears, etc. When, therefore, the term " organ " is used in this book it should be understood that both organs are meant.

Each hemisphere is divided into three parts or lobes ; the front, or forehead ; the rear lobe, or back-head ; and the middle lobe between the other two. The front lobe has its outlook, as it were, on the outer world, enabling us to obtain knowledge of men and things; to compare and arrange facts; and to invent and make what we need for the practical use of our knowledge.

SEAT OF MORAL POWERS

The upper part of the middle lobe, called the coronal region, because it lies under the crown of the head, is the seat of the moral powers, occupying the highest place, as they are meant to serve the highest ends and aims of man.

SEAT OF ANIMAL INSTINCTS

The lower part of this lobe, and the whole of that in the back-head, is devoted to the propensities, or those powers which, arising from natural impulses, simply produce desires or inclinations to bring about certain actions and no more. They give force and efficiency in all activities; adapt us to our fellows; and lead us to take care of ourselves. These have to do with natural things, and are closely related to the physical system; they are appropriately placed nearest the body, with which their connection is intimate through the spinal marrow and its branching nerves.

THE THREE CLASSES

It will thus be seen that the first division of the mental faculties and the organs of the brain through which they operate is into three grand classes:

1. The Propensities (or natural impulses).
2. The Thinking or Intellectual Faculties.
3. The Moral or Spiritual Sentiments.

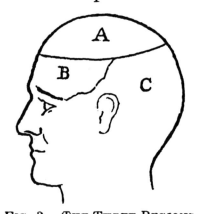

FIG. 3. THE THREE REGIONS
A—The spiritual region
B—The thinking faculties
C—The propensities

The way in which these are arranged, each in its special region of the brain, is shown in Figure 3.

The grand classes or orders of organs and faculties may each be divided into smaller groups, the *members of which bear a still closer relation to each other than to members of other sub-groups. These are shown in Figure 4.

1. THE PROPENSITIES

The region of propensities is divided into the

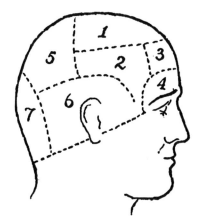

FIG. 4. THE ORGANS GROUPED
1—Moral sentiments
2—Semi-intellectual sentiments
3—Reason
4—Perceptive organs
5—Selfish sentiments
6—Selfish instincts or propensities
7—Social instincts or propensities

social and selfish groups. The social group includes those propensities which connect us with home and country and prompt us to love friends, relations, the members of the family circle, and congenial companions. Large Philoprogenitive- ness (or Parental Love) will lead a mother and father to love and care for their children. Large Conjugal Love, or Conjugality, will make the hus- band and wife desire the companionship of each other more than that of any one else. Other organs in this group are Amativeness, Adhesive- ness, and Inhabitiveness.

The office of the selfish group, on the contrary, is that of self-preservation. Such organs as Com- bativeness, Destructiveness, Alimentiveness, Vita- tiveness, Acquisitiveness, and Secretiveness fall naturally in this class, although some of these are necessary to economy and prudence.

2. THE THINKING, OR INTELLECTUAL, FACULTIES

These comprise such organs as Individuality, Form, Size, Weight, Color, Order, Time, Tune, Eventuality, Calculation, Locality, Causality, and Comparison. According to the growth and activ- ity of one or more of the intellectual faculties men show a bent toward certain professions.

Constructiveness, Ideality, Human Nature, Imitation, Mirthfulness, and Agreeableness form what is called the Semi-Intellectual Group. This class of organs is largely developed in the orator, the artist, the sculptor, the skilled mechanic, the poet, and the author, and gives the desire for self-improvement and a love for the beautiful in art and nature. It is elevating and refining in its influence, and acts in combination with the strictly religious group, to which it is closely related.

But it should be borne in mind that more than one class of organs is necessary to form these types. Thus, while the orator needs Sublimity, Ideality, Imitation, and Wit, which also belong to this group, he also requires faculties belonging to the other groups described, else his development is too one-sided to make him completely successful.

3. MORAL OR SPIRITUAL SENTIMENTS

The third division of the faculties, the religious group, has the highest office of all, and is made up of such organs as Conscientiousness, Hope, Veneration, and Benevolence. The devout Christian, the religious enthusiast, the adoring worshiper, the troublesome heresy hunter, and the Spiritualists, have their place in this division. Moralists, clergymen, and philanthropists also depend upon one or more of the organs found in this group for their marked traits of character.

CHAPTER V

PRACTICAL DIRECTIONS

BEFORE beginning the more detailed description of the various organs of the human brain, their special duties, and the influence which they exercise on character at different stages of development, we shall, in this chapter, give practical directions for their proper measurement, in order that the student may commence at once to put the knowledge which he gradually acquires into practical use.

The size of an organ is estimated by its length and breadth. Its length is measured by its distance from the medulla oblongata, or top of the spinal marrow, to the surface of the head.

A line drawn through the head, from the opening of one ear to that of the other, would, in the middle, pass close to, but a little in front of, the medulla; hence the length is measured from the line of the ear to the outside line of the skull.

An organ may be likened to a cone, turned upside down, like the letter V, with its point in the medulla, and its base at the surface of the brain. The broader the base and the longer the distance between it and the point, the greater will be the size, or the quantity of matter which it will contain. It is not, however, to be understood that the organs may be seen lying like so many cones. This is merely a convenient illustration of the way in which their size is estimated.

Nor are the organs separated by divisions in the brain corresponding to the lines shown in the illustrations; but each one, when large, gives to the skull a look like that pictured, so that the forms are not merely imaginary. The brain being soft, when the skull is opened the forms which the organs kept in life relax or change. The folds, however, differ enough in their size, appearance, and the direction in which they lie, to enable a good observer, acquainted with the subject, to tell an organ of propensity or sentiment from an organ of intellect.

The difference in growth between a large and a small organ, in those of the propensities and some of the sentiments, amounts to an inch and upward, and to a quarter of an inch in the organs of intellect.

THE FIRST PRINCIPLE

A healthy brain at a vigorous period of life is the proper subject for study. But as the first principle of the science is that the power or energy of mental operations bears a uniform relation, other conditions being equal, to the size of the organs, we must be careful not to confuse this quality of mind with that of simple action in the faculties. Size in the organ is an indication of power, and not at all of activity.

AN ILLUSTRATION

To make clear this difference between power or energy, and activity, we may take as an illustration those actors who are. noted for their solemn slowness of manner, both in movement and delivery, and yet who are splendidly gifted with power. By quiet methods they capture the sympathies and understanding of the audience at once, and sway it to laughter or tears as they will. This is a display of power. Many performers, on the other hand, are remarkable for quickness of action and elocution, who nevertheless are felt to be feeble and ineffective in arousing an audience to emotion. Activity is thus their distinguishing characteristic, with an absence of power. At the

bar, in the pulpit, and in the Senate, the same dis
tinction prevails.

Size a Measure of Power

Upon the principle stated, that size is a
measure of power, brains may be expected to
vary in their general size in proportion to the
degree of mental energy possessed. Our first
object, therefore, ought to be to find out the
size of the brain generally, in order to judge
whether it be large enough to admit of the
exhibition of ordinary vigor; if it be too small,
weak-mindedness or idiocy is an invariable consequence.

To Determine Kind of Power

The second object should be to learn the
relative proportions of the different parts, in
order to determine the direction in which the
power is greatest. If there is a greater quantity
of brain behind the ear than in front, and if the
base of the head is larger than the upper part,
it may be inferred that the lower faculties, or
animal propensities, rule the person under examination.

If, measuring from the opening of the ear to

the top of the head, the height be large, then the moral faculties must be well developed. If the space from the ear to the eyebrows be long, the seeing, or knowing faculties (*i. e.*, from the power they possess of collecting knowledge and of taking note of the existence and qualities of outside objects), are large. If the space from the ear not only to the eyebrows, but to the upper portion of the forehead, is large, and the forehead broad, in this case the faculties having to do with reflection, or the power to think and reason, will be found in great force and perfection.

The breadth of an organ is shown by its enlargement at the surface of the head. Hence if the line from the ear to the forehead (behind which are situated the organs of intellect) is much longer than from the ear backward, the intellect rules. On the other hand, if the forehead is very narrow, and the hind-head very broad, the animal organs, or propensities, are stronger.

The older phrenologists often used calipers to find the general size of the head, but not to indicate the dimensions of particular organs, for which purpose they are not adapted. Combe, in his treatise on Phrenology, gives the following measurements as the average size of twenty heads of men between twenty-five and fifty years of age, selected at random from many more measurements in his possession.

AVERAGE SIZE OF HEADS

From Philoprogenitiveness (marked 3 in Figure 5 [1], and corresponding to the swelling of the back part of the head) to Individuality (marked 27, and located in the middle of the lower part of the forehead)—in other words, from the most prominent part of the front to the most projecting part of the back-head—seven and four-eighths inches.

From the opening of the ear to the swelling of the back-head—four and three-eighths inches.

From the opening of the ear to Individuality—rather more than four and seven-eighths inches.

From the opening of the ear to Firmness (No. 16, Fig. 5) at the top of the head—rather more than five and seven-eighths inches.

From Destructiveness to Destructiveness (No. 9, Fig. 5)—in other words, the central breadth

[1] For these plates see Chap. VI, pages 80, 81, 82.

of the head—rather less than five and seven-eighths inches.

From Cautiousness to Cautiousness (No. 13, Fig. 5)—giving the breadth of the hind-head, rather less than five and six-eighths inches.

From Ideality to Ideality (No. 23, Fig. 7)—giving the breadth of the forehead—rather more than five and one-eighth inches.

These measurements were taken in length (from the back to the front of the head, from the ear to the front, and from the ear to the back); in height (from the ear to the top of the head); in breadth (on the forehead, at the centre of the head, and at the hind-head). They show the size of the head in these directions, but they are not given as indications of the dimensions of any of the phrenological organs.

It may be noted, in passing, that the average of these twenty heads is higher than is usually the case, because there were several large heads among them and none small.

After becoming familiar with the general size and form of heads, and learning to judge the proportions which the general mass of the several groups of organs bear to each other, the student may proceed to look for the individual organs, and in studying these, the real dimensions, and not the mere prominence of each organ, should be sought.

QUALIFICATIONS NECESSARY FOR PHRENOLOGY

Practice, with at least an average endowment of the organs of Form, Size, and Locality, is necessary to qualify a person to make observations with success. Individuals whose heads are very narrow between the eyes, and little developed at the top of the nose, where these organs are placed, find difficulty in making out the situations and little differences in the proportions of the several organs.

If one organ is of large growth and the neighboring organ very small, the larger organ shows an elevation ; but if the neighboring organs be developed in proportion, the surface is apparently smooth and no hump can be perceived. The student should learn from books, plates, and casts, and, if possible, personal instruction, to make out the form of each organ and its appearance when developed in different proportions to the others. The phrenological bust or picture shows only the places of the organs and their proportions in one head ; and it is impossible for it to show

more. The different appearances in all the
varieties of relative size must be discovered by in-
specting a number of heads; and especially by
contrasting instances of extreme development with
others of extreme deficiency. No adequate idea
of the foundation of the science can be formed until this is done. In cases of extreme size of single
organs, the form shown on a phrenological bust is
seen distinctly.

To Prove Its Truth

To prove Phrenology to be true, says Combe,
we do not, in general, compare an organ in one
head with the same organ in another; because it
is the prominence of particular organs in the same
head that gives the ruling power to single faculties in the individual; therefore in proving Phrenology we usually compare organs of the same
head. But in learning to observe, it is useful to
contrast the same organ in different heads, in order
to become familiar with its appearance in different sizes and combinations.

Value of Comparison

With this in view, it is proper to begin with the

larger organs; and two persons of opposite disposition in the special points to be compared ought
to be placed side by side and their heads observed.
Thus, if we take the organ of Cautiousness (see 13
in Fig. 6) we should examine its growth in those
whom we know to be remarkable for timidity,
doubt, and hesitation; and we should contrast its
appearance with that which it presents in individuals remarkable for boldness, and into whose
minds doubts and fears rarely enter. Or the
organ of Philoprogenitiveness in a person who is
passionately fond of children may be compared
with the same organ in another who regards them
as a great nuisance. No error is more to be
avoided than beginning with observation of the
smaller organs and examining these without a contrast.

THE SHAPING INFLUENCE OF SEX

In deciding upon the size of the organs, the difference between the sexes should be borne in mind,
as the heads of men and women are found to correspond to the different walks of life in which
men and women are best adapted to move.

Man, possessing by nature a larger frame, with
a temperament and body adapted to bear the bur-

dens of life, has also a form of head which plainly shows his sphere of action. In his head we find the organs which give energy and physical power larger than in woman, particularly Destructiveness, Combativeness, Imitativeness, Self-Esteem, and Firmness. His intellectual organs are larger, hence the greater width of his forehead; his head is much broader, but not so long, higher in the region of Firmness and Self-Esteem, but not so full in the moral and social organs.

In the average woman's head, on the other hand, we find larger Benevolence, Reverence (or Veneration), Conscientiousness, Inhabitiveness, Approbativeness, Adhesiveness, and Philoprogenitiveness. These give the fulness in the crown and back part of the head, and also the length noticeable in the heads of most of the sex. The head is long from the forehead back to Philoprogenitiveness, but narrower from ear to ear.

These differences correspond to the differences in their character. Man, with his strong intellectual and physical powers, is fitted to encounter the hardships, the dangers, the rude tempests, and the severe struggles through which he usually must pass in his encounters with the world. He needs sternness, courage, perseverance, self-confidence, and those qualities which fit him for a protector and shield for his more delicate companion.

But woman's influence arises from a different combination of organs. Her reign is the reign of love. She conquers by mildness, where man fails by force. She is at home in the social circle, where man is often ill at ease. She is the example and defender of morality and virtue, and wins by her gentle eloquence and charm where the sterner nature of man sometimes fails to convince. Her strong Adhesiveness and Philoprogenitiveness, her Hope, Spirituality, and Ideality, qualify her for the hard duties of the wife, the mother, the nurse, and the confiding friend.

Combinations of Size

Every person has all the mental organs, but they are combined in different degrees of relative size in various individuals ; and the operations of each are modified in some degree by the influence of those with which it is combined.

Three rules may be laid down for estimating the effects of differences in relative size, occurring in the organs of the same brain.

Rule 1

Every faculty desires gratification with a degree of energy proportionate to the size of its organ.

The individual will habitually indulge the faculties for which he has the largest organs.

If all the animal organs are large, and all the organs of the moral sentiments and intellect small, the individual will be naturally prone to animal indulgence in the highest degree, and disposed to seek satisfaction in the most direct way, and in the lowest pursuits.

If, on the other hand, the organs of the moral sentiments and intellect are larger than the rest, the individual will be naturally prone to moral and intellectual pursuits; such persons are " a law unto themselves."

Rule 2

Where large animal organs are combined with intellectual and moral organs, the animal organs will take their direction from the higher powers.

As there are three distinct kinds of faculties, Animal, Moral, and Intellectual, it may happen that several large animal organs are combined in the same individual with several moral and intellectual organs highly developed. The lower propensities will then take their direction from the higher powers; and such a course of action will be constantly followed as will be calculated to gratify these faculties whose organs are large.

If the organs of Acquisitiveness and Conscientiousness are both large, stealing might gratify Acquisitiveness, but it would offend Conscientiousness. Accordingly, the individual would endeavor to gratify both by acquiring property by lawful industry.

If, in an individual, Amativeness is very large, and Philoprogenitiveness, Adhesiveness, and Conscientiousness deficient, he will be prone to the most direct satisfaction of the animal appetite; if Conjugality is large, he will perceive that marriage affords the only means of pleasing the whole group of faculties.

If Benevolence, Self-Esteem, and Acquisitiveness are all large, giving charity may gratify the first; but unless the person is very rich, the act of parting with property may be disagreeable to the last two faculties; he would therefore prefer to gratify Benevolence by personal kindness; he would sacrifice time, trouble, influence, and advice to the welfare of others, but not personal possessions. If Benevolence were small, with the same combination, he would give neither money nor personal service.

The intellectual faculties will naturally tend to such employments as will satisfy the ruling propensities and sentiments. If the organs which give a genius for painting are combined with large Acquisitiveness, the individual would paint to become rich ; if combined with small Acquisitiveness, and large Approbativeness, he would probably labor for fame,—and starve while attaining it.

RULE 3

When all the organs appear in nearly equal proportions to each other, the individual, if left to himself, will exhibit opposite phases of character, according as the animal propensities or moral sentiments rule for the time.

That is, he will pass his life in alternate sinning and repenting. If outside influence is brought to bear upon him, his conduct will be greatly modified by it ; if placed, for example, under severe discipline and moral restraint, these will cast the balance, for the time, in favor of the higher sentiments ; if exposed to the influence of

evil associates, the animal propensities will probably obtain triumphant sway.

COMBINATIONS IN ACTIVITY

Where several organs are large in the same individual, they have a natural tendency to combine
in activity, and to prompt him to a line of conduct
designed to gratify them all. When, however,
all or the greater number of the organs exist
in nearly equal proportions, important practical
effects may be produced, by establishing combinations in activity among particular organs, or
groups of organs.

For example, if Individuality, Causality, Comparison, and Language are all large, they will naturally tend to act together, and the result of their
combined activity will be a natural talent for public
speaking or literary composition. If Language be
small, it will be extremely hard to establish such
a combination in activity, and the natural talent
will be small.

But suppose we take two persons, in both of
whom this group of organs is of an average size,
and train one to a mechanical employment, and
the other to the bar. In the latter, the reflecting
organs and that of Language will be trained to

act together, and the result will be an acquired ability in writing and debate; whereas, in the former individual, in consequence of the organ of Language not being accustomed to act in combination with those of intellect, this facility would be utterly wanting.

EFFECTS OF EDUCATION

It is by virtue of this principle that education produces its most important effects. If, for instance, we take two persons, in each of whom all the organs are developed in an average degree—and if one of them has been educated among persons of sordid and mercenary disposition—Acquisitiveness and Self-Esteem would then be cultivated in him into a high degree of activity; and self-interest and personal enrichment would be viewed as the great objects of life. If Approbativeness were trained to act with these faculties, it would desire distinction in wealth or power; if Veneration were trained to act in concert with them, it would take the direction of admiring the rich and the great; and, Conscientiousness not being greatly vigorous, would only suggest that such pursuits were unworthy, without possessing the power, by itself, of overcoming or controlling the whole combination against it.

If another person possessing the same development were trained in a moral and religious environment, where benevolence and justice toward men, and veneration toward God, were represented as the leading objects of human existence, the organ of Approbativeness, acting with this combination, would desire esteem for honorable and virtuous actions; and Acquisitiveness would be viewed as the means of satisfying these higher powers, but not as itself an object of the greatest importance. The practical conduct of the two individuals might thus be very different in consequence of this difference of training.

This principle is not inconsistent with the influence of size; because it is only in individuals in whom the organs are nearly equal in point of size, that such great effects can be produced by combinations in activity. In these cases the phrenologist, in estimating the effects of size, always inquires about the education bestowed.

Self-Improvement as a Modifying Cause

Even where certain organs, or groups of organs, as, for example, the propensities, show more than average development, their influence may be modified by right training or efforts at self-improvement. Thousands of instances might be cited where long continued exercise has caused organs deficient in size and power to grow, even after the person had arrived at the age of thirty years.

EXAMPLES

Spurzheim mentions the case of an English gentleman who, to test the truth of this statement, had a cast of his head taken, and then directed his close attention to some new pursuit. Each year for five years thereafter he had similar casts taken and, on comparing them at the end of that period, the first and last casts were found to differ so much that it was hard to believe they were taken from the same individual.

Another gentleman was told by a phrenologist at the age of twenty-four that his organ of Eventuality was so small as to show a depression, which accounted for his inability to remember facts, circumstances, anecdotes, incidents, etc. For four years he applied himself earnestly to the study of history, when it was found that the organ indicated had so developed as to fill up the hollow and increase the measurement around the head in that region.

Exercise gives power, and increases the size of any organ. By the same law which increases the muscles of the blacksmith's arm, makes our right arm stronger and larger than our left, that organ of the brain which we exercise most will grow most and be most powerful.

How to Find the Organs

It is comparatively easy to determine the locations of the perceptive organs and most of the others lying at the base of the brain by means of our diagrams and descriptions. The eyes, the eyebrows, or the little point on the skull just above the nape of the neck, called the occipital protuberance, furnish a convenient point of departure from which each may be reached with little chance for error. To find the exact situation of those lying farther from these fixed points, the beginner will require more practice, patient study and comparison.

Destructiveness

Drawing a line straight backward from the opening of the ear, you first cross Destructiveness (see Fig. 1, Frontispiece) which lies above and partly behind the ear. When large, there will be great width of brain between the ears, and a swelling out of the organ just above the opening of the ear, say the size of one-half of a common peach-stone. When small, the head will be narrow between the ears with no swelling at the point indicated.

SECRETIVENESS—SUBLIMITY AND CONSCIENTIOUSNESS—FIRMNESS

Next above this, and three-quarters of an inch from the top of the ear, lies the fore part of Secretiveness. Extending the line upward you pass over Sublimity and Conscientiousness, and at the top of the head strike the fore part of Firmness, which, when large, gives fulness to the crown. Taking this as another fixed point, the other organs on the middle line and each side of it can be readily found.

CONCENTRATIVENESS

Between Self-Esteem and Inhabitiveness, on this central line, is Concentrativeness which, being generally small in American heads, is usually

marked by a depression at that point, and is thus
easy to find.

CAUTIOUSNESS—IDEALITY AND MIRTHFULNESS

Cautiousness, which is another important point
to fix correctly in the mind, may be found by
drawing a perpendicular line upward from the
back part of the ear, and just where the head
begins to round off to form the top you will come
upon that organ. It often causes quite a prominence there. Forward of Cautiousness, and in
line with it, are Sublimity, Ideality, and Mirthfulness.

VENERATION—HOPE AND SPIRITUALITY

Veneration is situated between Firmness and
Benevolence in the centre of the top-head. When
this middle part rounds out and rises above the
parts immediately before and behind it, Veneration
is larger than Firmness and Benevolence. Below
Veneration are the two organs of Hope and Spirituality.

ACQUISITIVENESS AND CONSTRUCTIVENESS

Above Alimentiveness (just in front of the
upper part of the ear) and the fore part of Destruc-

tiveness, is Acquisitiveness, and forward of that organ, Constructiveness has its place.

PARENTAL LOVE—AMATIVENESS

To find Parental Love (or Philoprogenitiveness), draw a line backward from the outer angle of the eye to the centre of the back-head. An inch or a little less below this point is a hump called the occipital protuberance, which denotes by its degree of development the power of endurance and activity of the muscular system. On each side of this, and just below, Amativeness is located, giving breadth and thickness to the neck below and between the ears.

With these points fixed in mind, the student will be able to carry out for himself the plan indicated for finding the other organs, but he must bear in mind that there are slight modifications in their position on each head ; and he should therefore learn to distinguish the form and appearance of each by itself and as compared with the other organs in the same locality.

At first the student is often unable to perceive differences which, after a few months, become clear to him. It is related of Dr. Gall that he once received a box of skulls from the physician of the

House of Correction, at Graetz, in Styria. In unpacking them he was so struck with the extreme breadth of one of them in the fore part of the temples that he exclaimed, " My God, what a thievish skull!" Yet the physician himself had been unable to discover the seat of the organ of Acquisitiveness in that skull. His letter to Dr. Gall, sent with the box, and hitherto unopened, was found to contain this information: " The skull marked ——— is that of N——, an incorrigible thief." That was the identical skull which had drawn forth Dr. Gall's exclamation before he read the letter.

CHAPTER VI

THE ORGANS AND THEIR FUNCTIONS

WE will now take up a description of the various organs in the order of the list of definitions. The terms which may be used to denote the gradations of size in the different organs in a decreasing ratio are: Very Large, Large, Full, Moderate, Small and Very Small. It should be kept in mind that these terms indicate only the relative proportion of the organs to each other in the same head ; and not their absolute size, or their size in reference to any standard head.

THE PROPENSITIES
(*Social Group*)

1. AMATIVENESS
Physical Love or Propensity for the Opposite Sex

The organ of Amativeness is situated at the base of the back-head, in the cerebellum (little brain), as shown at 1, Fig. 5. It may be found by feeling on the middle line toward the base of the skull at the back part of the head until a small bony projection, called the occipital process, is dis-

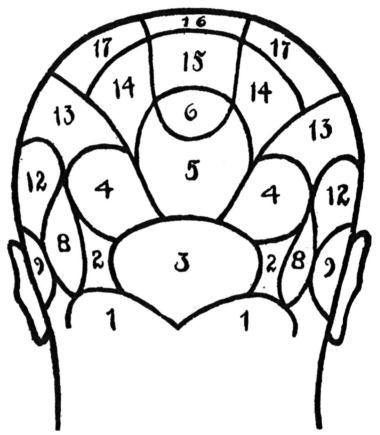

FIG. 5. ORGANS OF THE BACK HEAD

covered. Below this point and between two similar projections (the mastoid processes) behind the bottom of the ears, lies the organ in question. In other words, it is located directly over the nape of the neck and fills up the space between the ears be-hind. It gives thickness to the neck between the

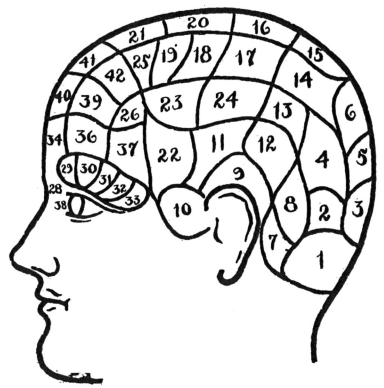

Fig. 6. ORGANS OF THE SIDE HEAD

ears when it is large, and spareness when small. (See Figs. 8 and 9.) When *large* (Fig. 8) it renders its possessor alive to the charms of the other sex, polite, affable, and free in their company, suc-

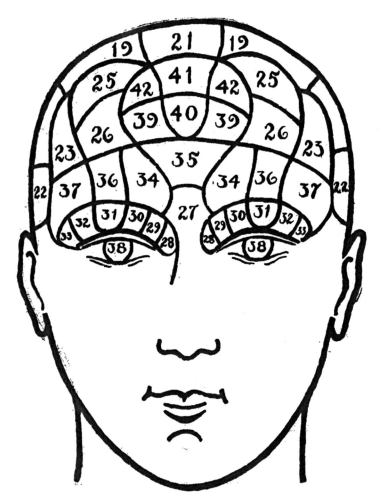

FIG. 7. ORGANS OF THE FRONT HEAD

cessful in gaining their confidence, and courageous in their defense. *Very large* gives a power and activity of sexual passion almost uncontrollable. *Full*, much love and tenderness for the opposite sex; yet, with activity great, excitability rather

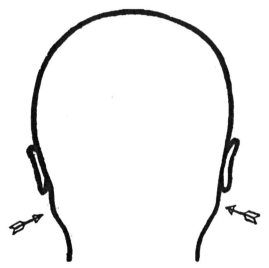

FIG. 8. AMATIVENESS, Large

than power. *Average*, love for the other sex and enjoyment in their society. *Moderate*, lack of sexual love, attentions to opposite sex, etc. *Small* (Fig. 9), little sex attraction or desire to marry. *Very small*, little or no liking for the opposite sex. In women it is usually less in proportion to the size of the brain than in men generally.

2. CONJUGALITY

Desire for a Permanent Union with the Opposite Sex—
The Pairing Instinct

Situated in the lower part of the back-head, just above Amativeness. Its position is shown by Fig. 10, also 2 in Fig. 5. Though this is closely

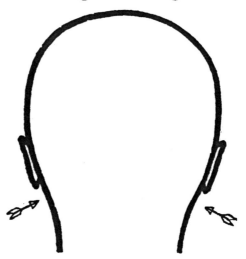

FIG. 9. AMATIVENESS, Small

related to Amativeness, it is a distinct faculty, and each may be exercised independently of the other. Thus a rake may be ruled by Amativeness, and yet have no desire to become allied lawfully to one woman. *Very large*, selects some one of the opposite sex as the sole object of love; longs always to be with that one; is true and faithful in wedlock, if mated in spirit; concentrates the whole soul on the beloved one, magnifying excellences and overlooking faults. *Large,* seeks but one sexual mate, and feels perfectly satisfied in the society of that one. *Full,* can love greatly, yet is capable of changing the object. *Average,* is disposed to

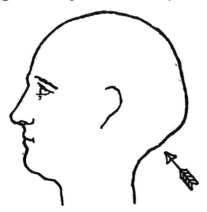

FIG. 10. CONJUGALITY

love only one for life; yet with Secretiveness and Approbativeness large, and Conscientiousness only full, is capable of coquetry. *Moderate,* is somewhat disposed to love only one, yet allows stronger faculties to influence that love. *Small,* has but little conjugal love, and seeks the promiscuous society and affection of the opposite sex, rather than a single partner for life. *Very small,* shows no desire for marriage.

3. PHILOPROGENITIVENESS

Love of Offspring, Attachment to Children, Pets, or any
Object of Care and Attention

Situated above the middle part of the cerebellum (see 3 in Fig. 5), and about an inch above the occipital process, this organ is one of the easiest to

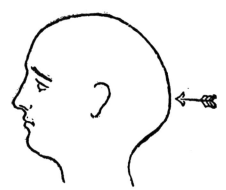

FIG. 11.   PHILOPROGENITIVENESS, Large

locate in the human head.   When large it projects like a portion of an ostrich egg.   Those who are flat and perpendicular in that region, instead of being delighted are annoyed by children.   It is usually smaller in men than in women, though sometimes found larger ; men so organized delight to nurse and care for children.   *Very large*, denotes a passionate fondness for children ; idolizes his own children ; is liable to overindulge them.

Large, (Fig. 11), feels strong parental love ; is devotedly attached and very kind to his own, if not to all children. *Full,* is tender, but not overindulgent ; fond of own children, yet cares little for others. *Average,* loves own children, yet not fondly ; dislikes those of others. *Moderate,* loves

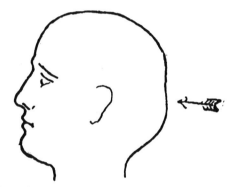

FIG. 12. PHILOPROGENITIVENESS, Small

own children mildly, but bears little from them. *Small,* (Fig. 12), feels little interest in even his own children. *Very small,* has no parental love ; dislikes all children. This organ when well developed gives a softness of manner in treating the feeble and delicate, even in advanced life ; and persons in whom this organ is large in combination with full Benevolence, are better fitted for the purpose of the sick-room than those in whom it is small.

4. ADHESIVENESS

Friendship, Attachments in General, the Bond of Brotherhood, the Foundation of Social Intercourse

Located on each side of the head, above Philoprogenitiveness (Fig. 5). *Very large*, loves friends with great tenderness and strength of feeling; will sacrifice almost anything upon the law of friendship. *Large*, is eminently social; an ardent, sincere friend; forms strong if not hasty attachments. *Full*, is highly social, yet not remarkably warm-hearted. *Average*, is quite friendly, yet will not sacrifice much for friends. *Moderate*, loves friends some, but self more. *Small*, is unsocial, cold hearted; likes and is liked by few. *Very small*, is a stranger to friendly, social feeling. This organ is generally larger in females than in males; hence the strength and durability of their love: it becomes an essential part of woman's nature.

5. INHABITIVENESS

Love of Home and Country; Attachment to Particular Localities; Desire to Dwell upon the Same Spot

Located immediately above Philoprogenitiveness (see 5 in Fig. 5), in the middle line of the back-head (Fig. 13). *Very large*, regards home as

the dearest, sweetest spot on earth; feels home-
sick when away; is eminently patriotic; thinks of
his native place with intense interest. *Large*, soon

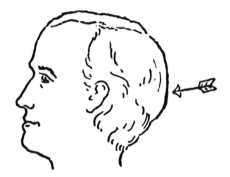

FIG. 13. INHABITIVENESS, Large

becomes strongly attached to the place in which
he lives; loves home and country dearly; leaves

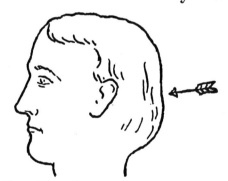

FIG. 13a. INHABITIVENESS, Small

both reluctantly; is unhappy without a home of
his own. *Full,* loves home well, yet does not

grieve much on leaving it. *Average*, forms some, though not strong, local attachments. *Moderate*, has some, yet not great, regard for home as such. *Small* (Fig. 13a), or *very small*, makes any place home.

6. CONTINUITY

Ability to Fix the Attention for a Length of Time upon any Object ; Concentration of Mental Action

Located above Inhabitiveness and Adhesiveness, and below Self-Esteem. When large, it gives a general fulness to that region ; and, when moderate or small, a marked depression is perceptible. (See 6 in Fig. 5.)

Very large, places his mind upon subjects slowly ; cannot leave them unfinished, cannot attend to more than one thing at a time ; is very tedious ; has great application, yet lacks intensity and point. *Large*, is able and inclined to apply his mind to one, and only one, subject for the time being, until it is finished ; changes his mental operations with difficulty. *Full*, is disposed to attend to only one thing at a time, yet can turn rapidly from thing to thing. *Average*, possesses this power to some, though to no great extent. *Moderate*, loves and indulges variety and change of thoughts, feeling, occupation, etc. ; rather lacks application ; has intensity, but not unity of mental action. *Small*, craves novelty and variety ; has little application ; thinks and feels intensely, but not long on anything ; jumps rapidly from premise to conclusion ; fails to connect and carry out his ideas. *Very small*, is satisfied only with constant change.

(*Selfish Group*)

7. VITATIVENESS

Love of Life; Desire to Live, Even Under the Most Unfavorable Circumstances

Believed to be located beneath and back of the

FIG. 14. VITATIVENESS
(Location shown by the star)

mastoid processes, behind the ear and forward of

Amativeness ; but there is more uncertainty about its situation than that of most other organs. (See 7 in Fig. 6 and Fig. 14.)

Very large, however wretched, shrinks from and shudders at the thought of death ; feels that he

FIG. 15. COMBATIVENESS, Large

cannot give up existence. *Large*, loves and clings tenaciously to existence for its own sake ; craves immortality and dreads annihilation, even though miserable. *Full*, desires life, but not eagerly, from love of it and of pleasure. *Average*, is attached to life and fears death, yet not a great deal. *Moderate*, loves life, but is not very anxious about living. *Small*, or *very small*, heeds neither life nor death, existence nor annihilation.

8. COMBATIVENESS

Propensity to Oppose; Feeling of Resistance; Bold-ness; the Source of Courage

Located about an inch and a half behind the top of the ear. (See 8 in Fig. 6.) To find it on the

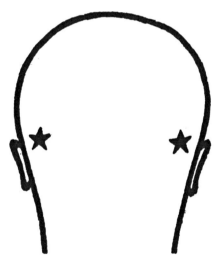

FIG. 16. COMBATIVENESS, Small

living head, draw a line from the outer angle of the eye to the top of the ear, thence straight back-ward for an inch and a half to an inch and three-quarters, and you will be over the place of the organ. When large it gives great breadth to the head at that point (as shown in Fig. 15).

Very large, is powerful in opposition, prone to dispute and attack; contrary; has a violent temper, governs it with difficulty. *Large*, is resolute and courageous, spirited and efficient as an opponent; loves debate. *Full*, seldom either courts or shrinks from opposition; when aroused is quite energetic; may be quick tempered, yet is not quarrelsome. *Average*, is usually mild, but when driven to it, defends his rights boldly. *Moderate*, avoids collision; is peace-loving and rather inefficient. *Small*, (Fig. 16), has feeble resistance, temper, and force; is cowardly. *Very small*, withstands nothing; is chicken-hearted; a thorough coward.

9. Destructiveness

Organ of Passion, Force, Severity, and Sternness

This organ is situated on both sides of the head, immediately over the external opening of the ear, extending a little forward and backward from it, and rising a trifle above the top or upper flap of the ear. (Figs. 17 and 18 show the form given to the skull when large and small.) Under the control of the higher sentiments and intellect, this faculty has a legitimate sphere of exercise.

Very large, when provoked is vindictive, cruel, disposed to hurt, take revenge, etc. ; bitter and implacable as an enemy ; very forcible and disposed to subdue or destroy the cause of his displeasure. *Full,* can, but is loath to, cause or witness pain

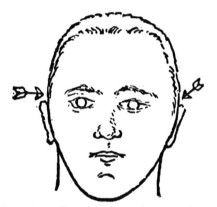

FIG. 17.   DESTRUCTIVENESS, Large

or death ; has sufficient severity, yet requires considerable to call it out. *Average,* has none too much force and indignation. *Moderate,* is mild, not severe enough ; when angry lacks power. *Small,* would hardly hurt any one if he could, or could if he would ; his anger is so feeble that it is derided more than feared. *Very small,* is unable to cause, witness, or endure pain or death.

10. ALIMENTIVENESS

The Desire or Appetite for Food and Drink

Located immediately in front of the upper part of the ear (10, in Fig. 6). To find it, take the upward and forward junction of the ear with the head as the starting point and draw a line half

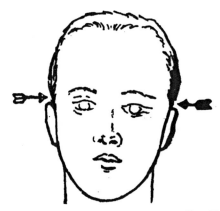

FIG. 18. DESTRUCTIVENESS, Small

an inch forward toward the eye, inclining a little downward, and you will be upon it.

Very large, sets too much store upon the indulgence of the palate; eats with keenest enjoyment. *Large*, has an excellent appetite, and a hearty relish for food and drink; is a good liver, not dainty. *Full*, has a good appetite, yet can govern it; is not greedy. *Average*, enjoys food well, but not very well; hence is particular as to what he eats. *Moderate*, has not a good nor very poor, but rather poor, appetite. *Small* or *very small*, is dainty, particularly about food; eats with little relish.

11. ACQUISITIVENESS

Propensity to Acquire Wealth; Love of Property, Without Regard to the End or Uses to which it may be Applied

Situated on the side of the head, next above Alimentiveness (11, in Fig. 6). To find, take the middle of the top of the ear as a starting point and move the finger directly upward an inch, and then horizontally forward the same distance, and it will rest directly over the organ.

Very large, is miserly, makes money his idol; is tempted to get it dishonestly; is sordid in his ideas and covetous. *Large*, has a strong desire to acquire property; is saving, close and particular in his dealings, devoted to money-making, trading, etc., and usually gets the value of his money. *Full*, values property, both for what it is and what it procures, yet is not penurious; is industrious and saving, yet supplies his needs. *Average*, loves money, but not greatly; can make it, but spends freely. *Moderate*, finds it more difficult

to keep than to make money ; desires it more to
supply wants than to hoard ; is hardly saving
enough. *Small*, will spend money freely, often
unwisely ; lays up little ; disregards the prices of
things. *Very small*, cannot be taught the value
of money.

12.   SECRETIVENESS

*Tendency to Conceal ; to Work in Secret ; Prudence in
the Management of Private Affairs*

Situated immediately above Destructiveness,
about an inch above the top of the ears (12,

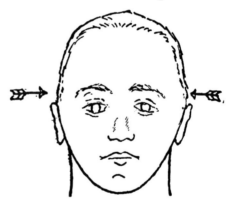

FIG. 19.   SECRETIVENESS, Large

in Fig. 6).   When this organ and Destructiveness
are both highly developed, there is a general fulness of the lower and middle portions of the side-
head (as shown in the outline, Fig. 19).

Very large, seldom appears what he is, or says what he means; often deceives; is mysterious, cunning, artful, given to double-dealing. *Large*, seldom tells his plans, opinions, etc.; is reserved and non-committal. *Full*, can keep to himself what he wishes to, yet is not cunning. *Average*, is not artful nor very frank; is generally open,

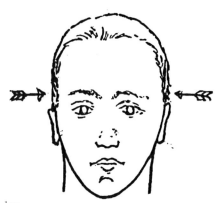

FIG. 20. SECRETIVENESS, Small

but can conceal. *Moderate*, is quite candid and open-hearted; loves truth; dislikes concealment, underhand measures, etc.; seldom employs them. *Small* (Fig. 20), speaks out just what he thinks; acts as he feels; does not wish to learn or tell the secrets of others, yet freely tells his own; is too plain spoken and candid. *Very small*, his thoughts and actions are thoroughly transparent.

CHAPTER VII

THE MORAL SENTIMENTS

(Selfish Group)

13. CAUTIOUSNESS

Sense of Fear, Apprehension of Danger, Anxiety about Consequences, Care, Solicitude

SITUATED above Combativeness and Secretiveness. (See 13, in Fig. 6.) To find, take the back part of the ear as the starting point and draw a

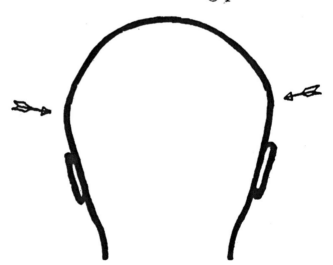

FIG. 21. CAUTIOUSNESS, Large

perpendicular line upward, and where the head begins to round off to form the top is the location of the organ. When large, the head is very broad at that point, while a deficiency gives quite another shape to the skull (as shown by Figs. 21 and 22).

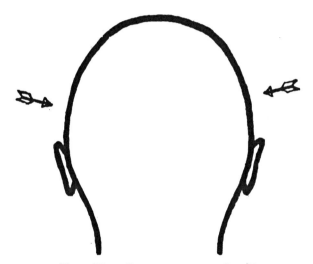

FIG. 22.   CAUTIOUSNESS, Small

Very large, hesitates too much; suffers greatly from groundless fears; is timid and easily frightened. *Large*, is always watchful, on the lookout, careful and anxious. *Full*, has prudence and forethought, yet not too much. *Average*, has some caution, yet hardly enough for success. *Moderate*, is rather imprudent, hence unlucky; liable to misfortune caused by carelessness. *Small*, acts impulsively; disregards consequences; fears nothing; is imprudent and often in " hot water." *Very small*, is without fear and forethought.

14. APPROBATIVENESS

Desire of Public Applause, Distinction or Fame; Love of Praise and Anxiety to Please

Approbativeness is located on the upper and back part of the top side-head, between Cautiousness and Self-Esteem, at the point marked 14 in Figure 5. When large it produces a remarkable fulness and breadth in the upper and back part of the head.

Very large, regards his character and honor as the apple of his eye; is often morbidly sensitive to praise and censure; very fond of show, fashion, praise, style, etc.; extremely polite and ceremonious. *Large*, sets great store by honor and character; is keenly alive to the praise, the frowns and smiles of public opinion; tries to show off to good advantage; is affable, ambitious, apt to praise himself. *Full*, desires and seeks popularity and feels censure, yet will neither deny nor trouble himself much to avoid either. *Average* enjoys approbation, yet will not sacrifice much to obtain it. *Moderate*, feels reproach some, yet is little affected by popularity or unpopularity ; may appreciate the applause that comes to him, yet will do little to obtain it. *Small*, cares little for pop-

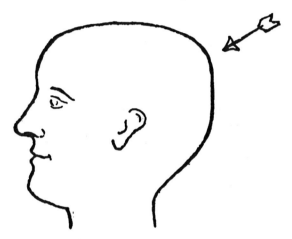

Fig. 23. Self-Esteem, Large

ular frowns or favors; feels little shame; disregards and despises fashion, etiquette, etc. ; is not polite. *Very small*, cares nothing for the opinion of the world.

15. Self-Esteem
Pride of Character and Self-Respect ; Confidence in One's Own Powers

The organ of Self-Esteem is situated at the back

part of the top-head, where the crown begins to decline toward the back-head. (See 15, Figs. 5 and 6.) When it is large, the head rises far upward and backward from the ear. (See Figs. 23 and 24.)

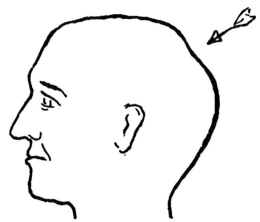

FIG. 24.   SELF-ESTEEM, Small

Very large, has unbounded self-confidence; endures no restraint; takes no advice; is rather haughty and imperious. *Large*, is high-minded and independent, self-confident, dignified, his own master; aspires to be and do something worthy of himself; assumes responsibility; does few petty things. *Full*, has much self-respect, pride of character, and independence. *Average*, respects himself, yet is not haughty. *Moderate*, has some self-respect and manly feeling, yet too little to give ease, dignity, and weight of character; is too trifling. *Small*, (Fig. 24), says and does trifling things; associates with inferiors; is not looked up to; lacks independence. *Very small,* is servile, low-minded, destitute of self-respect.

16. FIRMNESS

Decision of Character, Perseverance, and Strength of Will

Located near top of head, next higher than Self-Esteem and between that organ and Veneration. (See 16, in Figs. 5 and 6.)

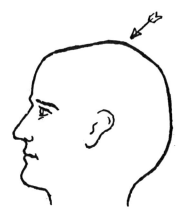

FIG. 25. FIRMNESS, Large

Very large, is wilful and tenacious of opinion; seldom gives up anything. *Large*, (Fig. 25), may be fully relied on; is set in his own way; hard to be convinced or changed at all. *Full*, has perseverance enough for ordinary occasions, yet too little for great enterprises; is neither fickle nor stubborn. *Average*, has some decision, yet too little for general success. *Moderate*, gives in too soon; changes too often and too easily; thus fails

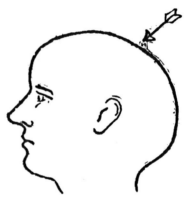

FIG. 26. FIRMNESS, Small

to accomplish what greater firmness would effect. *Small*, (Fig. 26) or *very small*, lacks perseverance; is too changeable to be relied upon.

(*Religious Group*)

17. CONSCIENTIOUSNESS

Sense of Right and Wrong; Conscience—the Moral Principle

Located on each side of Firmness, about three

inches above the opening of the ear, and about one and one-half inches from the middle line of the head. (See 17, in Fig. 6, also 23 and 24 in Fig. 6.) *Very large* is scrupulously exact in mat-

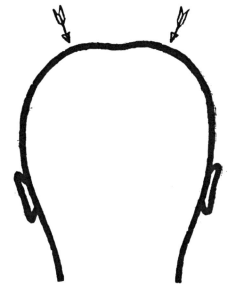

FIG. 27. CONSCIENTIOUSNESS, Large, with FIRMNESS, Small, gives this shape of skull

ters of right and perfectly honest in motive; always condemning self and repenting; makes duty everything, expediency nothing. *Large*, (Fig. 27), is honest, faithful, upright at heart; moral in feeling; loves, and means to speak, the truth; cannot tolerate wrong. *Full*, strives to do right,

yet sometimes yields to temptation; resists be-
setting sins, but may be overcome, and then feels
remorse. *Average*, has right intentions, but their
influence is limited. *Moderate*, has considerable
regard for duty in feeling, but less in practice;

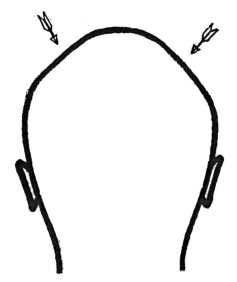

FIG 28. CONSCIENTIOUSNESS, Small

sometimes lets interest get the better of duty.
Small, (Fig. 28), has few conscientious scruples,
little regard for moral principle, justice, and duty.
Very small, does not feel the claims either of
justice or of duty.

18. Hope

Ardent Expectations ; Fond Anticipations ; Tendency to Look upon the Bright Side ; Optimism

Located forward of Conscientiousness, on each side of Firmness and Veneration. (See 18, in Fig. 6.)

Very large, has unbounded hope ; builds castles in the air. *Large*, expects, attempts, and promises a great deal ; is usually sanguine and cheerful ; though disappointed, hopes on still ; always views the brightest side of prospects. *Full*, is quite sanguine, yet realizes about what he expects. *Average*, has some, but reasonable, hopes ; is seldom elated. *Moderate*, expects and attempts but little ; succeeds beyond his hopes ; usually looks on the darker side of things. *Small*, is low-spirited ; easily discouraged, fears the worst ; magnifies evils ; lacks enterprise. *Very small*, expects nothing good ; is pessimistic ; has no hope of the future.

19. Spirituality

Internal Consciousness of Immortality and Faith in a Spiritual Existence

Situated immediately above Ideality. (See 19, in Fig. 6.)

Very large, is very superstitious; regards most things with wonder. *Large*, believes and delights in the supernatural, in dreams, ghosts, etc.; thinks many natural things to be supernatural. *Full*, is open to conviction; rather credulous; believes in divine Providence and premonitions. *Average*, believes some, but not much, in wonders, fore-

FIG. 29. VENERATION, Large

warnings, etc. *Moderate*, believes but little that cannot be accounted for, yet is open to conviction; is incredulous, but listens to evidence. *Small*, is convinced only with difficulty; believes nothing without evidence; is prone to reject new things without examination. *Very small*, believes little else than the evidence of the senses.

20. VENERATION

Respect for Religion and Sacred Things, and for Superiors

Situated in the middle of the top-head, between Benevolence and Firmness.

Very large, is eminent for piety, sincere devotion, religious fervor, and love of divine things. *Large,* (Fig. 29), loves to adore and worship God, especially through his works; treats equals with

FIG. 30. VENERATION, Small

respect, superiors with deference. *Full,* is capable of large religious fervor and devotion, yet is not habitually serious; generally treats his fellow men civilly. *Average*, may feel inclined for religious worship, yet have little respect for men. *Moderate*, disregards religious creeds and forms of worship.; is not serious or respectful. *Small*, (Fig. 30), has little feeling of worship, reverence, and respect. *Very small*, seldom if ever worships and adores God, and has no regard for superiors.

21. Benevolence

Generosity, Mercy, Good-will, Sympathy, Compassion, Kindness, and Desire to Make Others Happy

Situated in the middle of the fore part of the top-head, or summit of the forehead. When large it gives great elevation to this part. (See 21, in Figs. 6 and 7.)

Very large, does all the good in his power, and will sacrifice himself to help others. *Large*, is kind, obliging and helpful, mild and charitably inclined. *Full*, has a fair share of sympathy, compassion and charity. *Average*, sympathizes in some degree with the sufferings of others, yet is not inclined to put himself out much for the unfortunate unless he receives some return. *Small*, feels little kindness toward others, and is inclined to disregard their sufferings. *Very small*, indifferent to

FIG. 31. THE REV. LYMAN ABBOTT, D. D., LL. D.

the welfare of others, hard-hearted, and destitute of charity and common humanity.

The portrait of the Rev. Lyman Abbott (Fig. 31) shows a strong development of the moral and intellectual qualities (Fig. 31). Note the height of the front part of the top-head, showing large Benevolence. Conscientiousness, Veneration and Spirituality are also large. The head rises high above the opening of the ear, and is also lofty above the eye. Large Comparison, as shown by the rounded appearance of the middle part of the upper forehead, gives him the power to see the important points of a subject almost at once, while his large thinking faculties enable him to weave those points into effective argument. Large Constructiveness, forward of the top of the ears, between them and the corner of the eye (as shown in the right side of the portrait) enables him to put his thoughts into practical and easily understood forms, while Mirthfulness, Hope, and Causality seem to be well developed. These characteristics correspond with the known character of the man, whose influence among the intellectual classes of the American church has been very marked. Therefore, the portrait furnishes strong evidence that the principles of Phrenology are founded on laws as sound and correct as those of any science, and are not matters of mere guesswork.

(Semi-Intellectual Group)

22. CONSTRUCTIVENESS

Talent for Making, Contriving, Building, Planning and Inventing

Located forward of the top of the ears, between them and the corners of the eyes, immediately behind the temples. (See 22, in Figs. 6 and 7.) It is covered with a considerable mass of flesh or muscle, for which due allowance should be made in estimating its size.

Very large, is a mechanic or inventor of the first order. *Large,* shows great natural dexterity in using tools, executing mechanical operations, and working machinery. *Full,* has fair mechanical ingenuity, yet no great natural talent or desire to make things; will do well with practice; without it, little. *Average,* has some yet not great relish for and ability in using tools. *Moderate,* with large practice may use tools quite well, yet dislikes mechanical operations; owes more to training than to nature. *Small,* hates tools and is awkward and bungling in using them. *Very small,* has no mechanical skill or desire.

23. IDEALITY

Imagination, Taste, Refinement, and Love of the Fine Arts; Appreciation of Poetry and Oratory

Situated directly above Acquisitiveness and Constructiveness. (See 23, in Figs. 6 and 7.)

Very large, often gives rein to a vivid imagination; delights in fancy, and experiences rapture of feeling and enthusiasm. *Large,* has a lively imagination, great love of poetry, eloquence, good style in fiction, the beauties of art and nature. *Full,* has refinement of feeling and expression without sickly delicacy; some love of poetry, yet not a vivid imagination. *Average,* has some taste, though not enough to influence him much. *Moderate,* has some, but not much, imagination; is rather plain in expression, manners, and feeling; cares little or nothing for poetry or finery of any kind. *Small* or *very small,* lacks taste, niceness, refinement, and delicacy of feeling.

24. SUBLIMITY

Delight in Sublime Thoughts and Scenes, and Love of Grandeur Generally

Situated on the side-head directly above Acquisitiveness and behind Ideality. (See 24, in Fig. 6.) Many phrenologists do not recognize it as a distinct organ, but believe its supposed functions to be fully covered by Ideality. After giving the subject much attention, however, the Messrs. Fowler were well satisfied that it should take rank among separate organs.

Very large, has a passionate admiration of the wild and romantic, and feels sublime emotions while contemplating the grand or awful in nature. *Large*, admires and enjoys beautiful scenery, hence is fond of traveling. *Full*, enjoys magnificent scenes well, yet not remarkably so. *Average*, sometimes yet not always experiences this feeling. *Moderate*, has some though not vivid emotions of this kind. *Small* or *very small*, discovers little to awaken this feeling.

25. IMITATION

The Power of Imitating and Describing Anything Seen or Heard

Situated on the side of the top-head, between Ideality and Benevolence. (See 25, in Figs. 6 and 7.) When it is large, and Benevolence only moderate, the fore part of the top-head is nearly level; with Imitation and Benevolence both large, the outline at that point is curved (as shown in Fig.

32). When Benevolence is large and Imitation small, the form is like that presented in Fig. 33.

Very large, has a pronounced theatrical taste and talent; can impersonate any one or imitate,

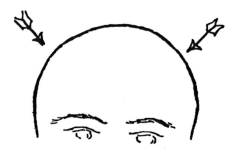

FIG. 32. IMITATION AND BENEVOLENCE, Both Large

describe, or relate almost anything heard or seen. *Large*, is easily able to imitate the tones and gestures of others. *Full* or *Average*, will seldom

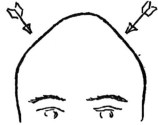

FIG. 33. IMITATION, Small ; BENEVOLENCE, Large

succeed remarkably well in mimicry, but will be able, with perseverance, to perform what others do with considerable success. *Moderate*, will seldom attempt to imitate ; cannot relate with much effect what he hears. *Small* or *very small*, has little or no ability in this line; will often spoil a good anecdote in the relation, and will succeed better in some calling where this faculty is not required.

26. MIRTHFULNESS

Love of Fun, Wit, Disposition to Joke, to Look at Things in a Humorous or Ludicrous Light

This organ is situated on the side of the upper part of the forehead, between Causality and Ideality. When large, it gives breadth to the upper region of the forehead. (See 26, in Figs. 6 and 7.)

Very large, is apt at turning everything into ridicule, throws constant sallies of wit; is too facetious and jocose. *Large*, has a quick, keen perception of the ludicrous; makes a great amount of fun, often too much for his own good; is quick at repartee; smiles often; laughs heartily at jokes. *Full*, has much mirthful feeling; makes and relishes jokes well. *Average*, perceives jokes, and relishes fun, but is not good at making much. *Moderate*, has some witty ideas, yet lacks quickness at conceiving, and tact in expressing them; is usually quite serious. *Small*, makes little fun; is slow to perceive, still slower to make jokes; seldom laughs. *Very small*, has few if any witty ideas or conceptions.

CHAPTER VIII

INTELLECTUAL FACULTIES

(Perceptive Group)

27. INDIVIDUALITY

Memory of Particulars, of Individuals, Power of Observation, Desire to See and Examine

THE organ of Individuality is situated in the centre of the lower part of the forehead, immediately above the top of the nose (Fig. 34). When large, it produces breadth, projection, and descent between the eyebrows at that part. When small, the eyebrows approach closely to each other, and lie in a nearly horizontal line.

Very large, has an insatiable desire to see and know everything; extraordinary observing powers; is eager to witness every passing event. *Large*, has a great desire to know, investigate, examine, and experience; quick of perception; sees what is transpiring, and what should be done.

FIG. 34. INDIVIDUALITY

Portrait of Tom L. Johnson, three times Democratic Mayor of the Republican city of Cleveland. Note the development directly above the top of the nose.

Full, has fair observing powers, and desire to see things. *Average*, has some yet no very great curiosity. *Moderate*, is rather deficient, yet not noticeably so, in observing power and desire. *Small*, is slow to see things; attends little to particulars. *Very small*, sees scarcely anything; regards everything in the mass.

28. FORM

Power of Judging of the Shape and Configuration of Objects—Memory of Persons and Faces

Located between the eyes, the size of the organ being in proportion to the width between them. (See 28 in Figs. 6 and 7.) In those who have it large, the eyes are wide apart, and vice versa.

Very large, never forgets the form, countenance, etc., of persons and things seen; has excellent eyesight. *Large*, notices and for a long time remembers faces, forms, and appearance of persons and animals; knows by sight many whom he may be unable to name. *Full*, has fair ability at remembering faces, forms, etc. *Average*, recalls forms and faces well, but not very well. *Moderate*, must see persons several times before he can recollect them. *Small* or *very small*, has a miserable memory of persons, looks, shape, etc. ; fails to recognize even those he sees often.

29. Size

Ability to Judge Magnitude, Distance, Height, Width, Dimensions, etc.

Located in or beneath the brow next to the nose, on each side of Individuality. (See 29, in Figs. 6 and 7.)

Very large, readily perceives a difference in the dimensions of different objects ; judges correctly of the weight of things by their size ; cannot endure inaccuracy. *Large*, has an excellent eye for measuring proportions, size, height, angles, and weight. *Full*, can measure ordinary and familiar distances well, yet shows no remarkable natural talent for it. *Average*, measures bulk with fair, though no great, accuracy. *Moderate*, is rather deficient in measuring by the eye ; with practice may do fairly well in short, but fails in long, distances. *Small*, judges of the relative size, weight, and proportions very inaccurately. *Very small*, will be liable to err in the size of every object ; will not be able to trust the eye for measuring, but must apply the rule ; therefore will fail in most mechanical pursuits.

30. Weight

Sense of Resistance, Ability to Support the Centre of Gravity, and Judge of the Resistance of Bodies

This organ lies next to that of Size, on the ridge of the eyebrows. When, large, it sometimes depresses the eyebrow at that point. (See 30, in Figs. 6 and 7.)

Very large, has this power to a wonderful extent. *Large*, can walk on high and narrow places; hold a steady hand, throw a stone or ball, and shoot straight. *Full*, keeps his centre of gravity well, but ventures little. *Average*, balances himself fairly well in ordinary cases, yet has no great natural talent in this respect. *Moderate*, maintains his centre of gravity rather poorly. *Very small*, will be liable to stumble or fall when walking; will be dizzy on high places; will not exce: as a skater or a marksman.

31. Color

Perception of Colors ; Ability to Distinguish the Different Shades and Recall Them

Occupies the precise centre of each eyebrow. (See 31, in Fig. 7.) The ordinary indication of its full development is the regular arching of the brow ; but sometimes the brow is pushed forward and made very prominent at that point. When large, it also gives a peculiar appearance of fulness to the upper eyelid.

Very large, extraordinary talent for detecting, remembering, and mixing colors. *Large*, has talent for comparing, arranging, mixing, applying, and recalling colors; is delighted with paintings. *Full*, with practice, compares and judges colors well; without it, does not excel. *Average*, can distinguish and recall colors, yet seldom takes particular notice of them. *Moderate*, aided by practice can discern and compare colors, yet owes less to nature than to art; seldom notices colors unless obliged to, and then soon forgets them. *Small*, seldom observes the color of one's hair, dress, etc.; cannot describe persons by what they wear, or compare colors apart. *Very small*, can tell white from black, but little more.

32. ORDER

System, Ability to Judge of the Fitness and Suitability of any Arrangement ; Desire to have a Place for Everything, and Everything in its Place

The organ of this faculty is placed under the eyebrow, between Color and Number. (See 32, in Figs. 6 and 7.) As it occupies only a small space, there is difficulty in observing it without consider-able experience.

Very large, is very precise and very particular to have everything just right; is worried by disor-der. *Large,* has a place for everything; is sys-tematic; can even find in the dark what he alone uses. *Full,* likes order; takes much pains to keep things arranged. *Average,* appreciates order, yet not enough to keep it. *Moderate,* likes, but does not keep, order. *Small* or *very small,* lacks neat-ness, and is inclined to delay; unreliable in keep-ing promises; is not worried by disorder.

33. NUMBER

Ability to Judge of the Relation of Numbers, Power to Reckon in the Head, to Excel in Mental Arith-metic

Located on the outside of Order, at the outer angle of the brow. (See 33, in Figs. 6 and 7.) When very large it gives the brow an arched or overhanging appearance.

Very large, has a natural talent for reckoning even complicated sums in the head; delights in doing so. *Large,* can add, subtract, divide, and multiply in the head with facility; de-lights and excels in arithmetic. *Full,* aided by rules and practice, may reckon figures well, but not without such aids. *Average*, by practice and rules, may learn figures quite well, but has no great love for them. *Moderate*, does sums in his head rather slowly and inaccurately. *Small*, is dull and incorrect in adding, dividing, etc., and dislikes arithmetic. *Very small*, can do little more than count correctly.

34. LOCALITY

Memory of the Relative Position of Objects, of Roads and Places ; Fondness for Geography

Located over the organs of Size and Weight, and on each side of Eventuality. (See 34, in Fig. 7.)

Very large, never forgets the appearance, location, or geography of any place he is ever in ; is passionately fond of travel and scenery. *Large*, recalls distinctly the looks of places, and seldom loses himself even in the dark ; has a strong desire to travel and see places. *Full*, remembers places well, yet is liable to lose himself in a city or forest. *Average*, has a fair though not excellent recollection of places. *Moderate*, recalls places rather poorly ; sometimes gets lost. *Small* or *very small*, seldom observes where he goes or finds his way back without assistance.

(Literary Group)

35. EVENTUALITY

Power of Recollecting Facts ; Memory of Circumstan-ces, Anecdotes, Incidents, Historical Facts, etc.

Located in the middle of the forehead above Individuality, and when large gives to that part of the head a rounded fulness. (See Fig. 35.)

Very large, never forgets any occurrence, even

FIG. 35. EVENTUALITY, Large
Location at A

though trifling; has a constant thirst for information and experiment ; commands an astonishing amount of ready information. *Large,* has a clear, retentive memory of historical facts, what he has seen, heard, and read, even in detail. *Full,* recalls leading events and interesting particulars, and has a good memory of occurrences, yet forgets less important details. *Average*, has only a fair memory of occurrences. *Moderate*, recalls things in the mass, but not details; is rather forgetful. *Small*, has a treacherous, confused memory. *Very small*, forgets almost everything.

36. TIME

Recognition of the Passing Moments ; Ability to Measure Time and Ability to Remember the Length of Time Between Given Events

Located just above the middle of the eyebrow, between Eventuality and Tune.

Very large, remembers with wonderful accuracy the time of occurrences ; is punctual in keeping appointments; tells the time of day by intuition. *Large*, tells dates, time of day, etc., well. *Full*, recalls, but not precisely, when things occur. *Average*, notices and remembers dates, time, etc., some, but not very well. *Moderate*, is rather poor at remembering dates and the lapse of time. *Small*, can seldom remember when things occurred; forgets dates. *Very small*, is liable to forget even his age.

37. TUNE

Sense of Harmony in Music ; Ability to Learn and Remember Tunes

The organ of Tune is situated on the side of the forehead just above the outer corner of the eyebrow next to Time. (See 37, in Figs. 6 and 7.) A great development of the organ enlarges the sides of the forehead; but its appearance varies according to the direction and form of the convolutions. Great practice is necessary to be able to observe this organ successfully. Beginners should place together a person possessing a genius for music and another who can scarcely distinguish between any two tunes, and mark the difference in development at the point named. The superior development of the former will be seen at a glance.

Very large, learns tunes by hearing them sung once or twice; shows natural skill and spends much time in making music; sings from the heart and with melting pathos. *Large*, easily catches tunes; learns to sing, and to play on instruments by ear; delights in singing; has a correct musical ear. *Full*, can learn tunes by ear well, yet needs notes to play very well. *Average*, likes music; with practice, may perform tolerably well. *Moderate*, aided by notes and practice may sing and play,

FIG. 36. TIME AND TUNE, Large

TIME is located just above the middle of the eyebrow, while TUNE has its place just above the outer angle of the brow. Both together give the broad appearance to the forehead in the above portrait of the late Edward Grieg, rated by a critic as " one of the few immortals in music."

yet it will in both cases be mechanical; lacks that soul and feeling which reaches the heart. *Small,* learns to sing or play either by ear or by note with great difficulty; sings mechanically and without emotion or effect. *Very small,* can hardly tell one tune or note from another. (See Fig. 36.)

38. LANGUAGE

Memory of Words or Arbitrary Signs; Ability to Retain the Language of Another

Located back of the eye, and will be recognized by the fulness of that organ, or by the swollen appearance above and below the eye. Sometimes the eyes not only project, but are also depressed, when the under eyelid presents a sort of sack or roll, or appears swollen. (See Fig. 37.)

Very large, has a natural and astonishing command of words, eloquence of expression, and verbal memory; quotes with ease; is an incessant talker; has too many words. *Large,* is a free, easy, ready, fluent talker and speaker; uses good language; commits to memory easily; seldom hesitates for words. *Full,* commands a fair share of words, yet uses familiar expressions; is neither fluent nor the reverse; when excited expresses himself freely, yet not in a brilliant way. *Average,* can com-

FIG. 37. LANGUAGE

This is the portrait of Dr. Zamenhof, the inventor of Esper
auto. Note the large eyes, behind which this organ is located.

municate his ideas fairly well, yet finds some difficulty in doing so ; uses common words; can write better than talk. *Moderate*, often hesitates for words ; employs too few ; may write well and speak foreign languages accurately; but is not an easy, fluent speaker. *Small*, employs only few words, and those are commonplace ; in speaking, hesitates much ; is barren in expression; commits to memory slowly. *Very small*, can hardly re member the use of words.

(*Reflective Group*)
39. CAUSALITY

Disposition to Search Out the Cause of Every Effect, to Investigate, to Argue as to the Why and Wherefore of Everything

Situated on the upper part of the forehead, on each side of Comparison, which occupies the centre. (See 39, in Fig. 7.) The two together, when both are large, give great fulness to that portion of the forehead.

Very large, is endowed with a deep, strong, original mind, powerful reasoning faculties, great vigor and energy of thought, first-rate judgment, and great intellect. *Large*, plans well ; can think clearly and closely ; is always inquiring into the why and wherefore, the causes and explanation of things; always gives and requires a reason; has by nature excellent judgment, good ideas, and a strong mind. *Full*, has an active desire to ascertain causes, yet not a deep, original, cause discovering and applying mind. *Average*, has some, but not great ability to plan and reason. *Moderate*, is rather slow of comprehension; deficient in adapting means to ends; has not good ideas or judgment. *Small*, has a weak mind; cannot think or contrive. *Very small*, has little idea of the connection between cause and effect; is a natural fool.

40. COMPARISON

Ability to Compare and Judge of the Quality of Different Things, to Discover Resemblances, and to Perceive Differences

Situated in the upper part of the forehead in the middle line between the two sides, and usually just below the roots of the hair, the bottom being about the centre of the forehead (Fig. 38).

Very large, has an extraordinary amount of critical wisdom, comparing and illustrating power. *Large*, has a happy talent for comparing and illustrating, criticizing and arguing from similar cases. *Full*, illustrates and discriminates well, but not remarkably so. *Average*, perceives striking similarities ; illustrates fairly well. *Moderate*, may see obvious similarities, yet overlooks others. *Small* or *very small*, has little of this power.

Not Grouped

The organs of Human Nature and Agreeableness were not recognized by the older phrenolo-

Fig. 38.　Comparison, Large (C)
This figure also shows Small Eventuality and
Large Individuality, at A and B, respectively

gists, but were definitely established and located by the Fowlers. By them they were placed under the Semi-Intellectual Group.

41.　Human Nature

Perception of Character and Motives
Located on the middle line of the forehead

between Comparison and Benevolence. (See 41, in Fig. 7.)

Large or *very large*, perceives the character and motives of men from their physiognomy, conversation, dress, etc. ; is suspicious and seldom deceived ; has a natural understanding of human nature. *Moderate* or *Small*, seldom suspects others ; is easily imposed upon ; learns to read human nature slowly ; does not know well how to take men ; lacks tact in dealing with them.

42. AGREEABLENESS

Ability to Make Oneself Agreeable

Situated on the upper edge of the forehead. It lies directly over the inner angle of the eye, and about two inches above the ridge of the eyebrow. (See 42, in Fig. 7.)

Large or *very large*, readily wins confidence and affection, even of enemies ; can say and do hard things without creating resentment ; obtain favors, and get along well. *Average* or *Full*, neither excels nor is deficient in this respect *Moderate* or *Small*, is deficient in the power described ; says pleasant things unpleasantly and does not succeed in winning friends.

CHAPTER IX

TEMPERAMENT AS A MODIFYING CAUSE

ONE of the arguments often used against the claim that mental ability can be determined by the size of the brain is the fact that men with small heads sometimes accomplish more than those who have heads of much greater size. This is true, while in no way disposing of the claims of phrenology, for the following reasons.

Taken as a whole, the head of a man may be small, and yet he may possess a powerful intellect owing to the fact that in him the region of the propensities, or sentiments, or of both, are undeveloped ; while the anterior (front) lobe of the brain, in which the intellectual organs are located, is large. The small size of the organs through which act the vital and animal faculties, therefore, give him a skull that is perhaps smaller than the average, although his other organs are of normal or more than normal size.

It consequently follows that a small head is

by no means a sure sign of lack of intellect, or
vice versa. And it will usually be found that
where the forehead, or front lobe, is very large,
and the other parts small, the intellectual power
is notable, but not the force to use it to good
advantage. The person lacks energy because of
the weakness of the vital organs. Men with
small heads may be brilliant, acute, and in particular directions strong, but they are not usually
profound or commanding. On the other hand,
men with large heads are often dull, if not stupid,
on account of low organic quality. Both high
quality and large size are essential to the highest
order of power, whether of body or mind.

After all, these exceptions only prove the rule,
for distinguished men of all ages, like Washing-
ton, Gall, Franklin, Webster, Beecher, and others,
all possessed large heads, and few instances can
be found where a decidedly great man has
possessed a really small head. The phrenologist
is therefore right in declaring that large mental
powers depend upon the size of the brain. All
the organs must not only be large, but they must
be in a constant state of activity.

Applying this law to distinct parts, we find
that in those men who possess extraordinary

faculties of whatever kind, the organs through which these faculties function always show a corresponding degree of development. In order to have a really good head each part must be full. (Fig. 39 shows a well-balanced head, and

FIG. 39.   FIG. 40.

Fig. 40, that of Dr. Gall, with large reflective and full perceptive faculties.)

HEALTH

The health of the brain should also be taken into consideration. Disease often makes such havoc in the brain that its natural strength or tone is entirely lost. Vice and excesses of any kind may have such an influence upon it that it becomes inactive and greatly loses its power until insanity or idiocy results. In other instances, the stomach is so feeble that it is not able to manufacture a sufficient quantity of blood to supply the brain with its proper nourishment; this causes slowness in the mental operations, giving indications of dullness and stupidity not justified by the development of the several organs. Such cases are exceptions to the general rule that size is the measure of power, because the conditions are not equal.

QUALITY

The quality of the brain, in which there is as much difference as there is in the bones or other parts of the body, should also be taken into account. In infancy the brain is soft, resembling a fluid almost as much as a solid. At this period the mental faculties are weak. But as the brain approaches maturity it gradually becomes more compact, has more tenacity, and the powers of the mind are found to keep pace with this gradual change. When the brain is not subjected to improper influences it continues to increase in size and weight until the age of complete maturity. Not until then is it fully developed, bringing with it a corresponding strength of mind.

Precocious Children

Those exceptional cases in which the brain matures early, due to continued exercise of the mind in childhood, seldom arrive at that degree of perfection found in those who are not thus forced along. Precocious children are usually not long lived. They reach maturity earlier, but seldom endure as long as less brilliant children. They are like tropical plants which come to a quick growth, bloom brilliantly for a short time, and then rapidly wither and die. It has long been observed that those minds remarkable for strength and endurance belong to individuals who in youth were not remarkably promising. In early life the vital powers of the latter were used by the body to lay a good physical foundation; when this was accomplished, and the body had attained its full growth, the vital energy was centered upon the brain. Thus their later mental growth was attended by a constitution capable of great endurance, a brain well sustained by pure, rich blood, and a consequent soundness of mind. A lion is strong because his muscles, ligaments, and bones are dense and tough. It is the same in man as in animals, in brain as in muscle. Real greatness can exist only where the bulky, compact brain is combined with strong nerves, and a dense, tough, firmly knit body.

It happens frequently that the brain, even in adults, is only little advanced beyond the ordinary condition of the brain of youth, and the powers of the mind correspond with the state of the brain.

It is highly important for the phrenologist to consider this condition, as two heads may be found of the same general size and shape, in one of which the quality of the brain is fine and compact, in the other coarse and watery. Now such persons would present very different characters.

RACIAL INFLUENCES

But how, asks the student, can we discover the quality of the brain? The answer is, by signs which indicate the temperaments. To a large extent, though not wholly, these indicate important constitutional qualities. There are some constitutional qualities which can be known only by knowing the full history of the stock, or race, from which the individual descended. Combe declared that he had observed a certain feebleness in the brain, indicating itself by weakness of mind without derangement, in individuals born in India

of an English father and a Hindu mother. He
had also noticed feebleness and sometimes irregu-
larity of action in the brains of individuals, not
insane, but who belonged to a family in which insanity abounded.

In a general way, however, the temperaments
afford a fairly accurate index to the condition of
the individual brain, and when making a phrenological examination these should always be taken
into account. The next chapter will show how
these are determined, and to what extent they influence the distinguishing traits of human character.

CHAPTER X

THE TEMPERAMENTS

TEMPERAMENT may be roughly defined as the quality and power of the mental and physical organs of the human body. In other words, it is the mixture of various qualities which make up the natural constitution of a person. When we say a man has a strong constitution we mean that these qualities are so combined as to give him the power to resist disease, to endure hardships, and to work hard without tiring easily. On the other hand, individuals with a weak constitution have little power of resistance, are not adapted to much hard labor, and are not fitted for anything demanding long continued effort, either mental or physical. Just as different woods vary in their strength and resistance because of the fineness or coarseness of their grain and the softness or toughness of their fibre, so do human bodies. Soft pine would make a poor handle for an axe, a hammer, or a pick, because it splits too easily to stand the hard usage to which these tools are put; but for other purposes it answers very well. Things are of value according to the grade or degree of quality which they have—whether they are hard or soft, dense or spongy, weak or strong.

In human beings this ruling quality is said to form the temperament. It is usually the result of different qualities acting together, the whole making up the constitution.

Persons differ a great deal in this regard. Few can be found whose make-up is exactly the same in bone and muscle elements, nerve power, circulation, or their power to digest and derive nourishment from the food which they eat. They may indeed be alike in some of these respects, but not in all. In just so much as a man differs from his fellows, in just that much may he be said to have a temperament of his own.

But once in a while we find two men who are much alike in this regard, and knowing the degree of mental and physical force in the one we can judge of the strength or weakness of the other.

The temperaments, as understood and applied by the older phrenologists in the study of character, were described as four—The Lymphatic, the Sanguine, the Bilious, and the Nervous.

These terms were founded on the degree of ruling power exercised by the stomach, the lungs, the liver, and the brain. Where either rules, it gives its peculiar tone to the mind and body.

THE LYMPHATIC TEMPERAMENT

may be known by the following signs. The skin presents a white or milk-like appearance; the hair is usually light, and the eyes light and dull. The form is round, and the stomach prominent. The flesh and muscles are soft, and the circulation of the blood slow and feeble; the movements of the body and brain, as a part of the physical system, are consequently slow and languid. Taking their tone from the body the mental operations are sluggish and weak.

THE SANGUINE TEMPERAMENT

This is shown by blue eyes, light or chestnut hair, fair skin, well defined form of moderate plumpness; a ruddy, lively countenance, strong and frequent pulse, and a well developed chest. The heart is large, the lungs strong, thus keeping the blood in good condition. People of this temperament dislike confinement, and have a fondness for exercise. They are ardent, fond of action, and impressible, and their brain shares the general vigor of the system.

Bilious, or Muscular, Temperament

The signs of this temperament are large muscles; a strong, well-built frame; hair usually coarse and black; black eyes, and skin of a dark yellow or brown hue. The flesh is firm and the bones large. The countenance shows strong, marked, and decided features. These qualities give endurance of body and mind, and indicate great activity, energy, and power.

The unusual activity of the nervous system gives rise to the

Nervous Temperament

indicated by light, thin hair, a slender, somewhat spare body, rapid muscular action, and a skin of fine texture. The eyes are usually dark and the features sharp; the countenance pale and the health delicate. The whole nervous system, including the brain, is usually energetic, and the mental operations quick and powerful.

Combination of Temperaments

The temperaments are seldom found pure, but are combined in various ways, as the Nervous with the Bilious or the Sanguine, called the Nervous-Bilious, or the Nervous-Sanguine. The most favorable temperament for physical labor is the Sanguine-Bilious; for mental effort the Nervous-Bilious combined with a share of the Sanguine.

Size is a measure of power in different individuals only when the temperaments are alike—and when all the other conditions are equal. Hence in deciding by this rule, judgment must be exercised, or we are liable to make mistakes.

To sum up, in comparing brains we should always first decide on the temperaments; because two brains may be of the same size; but if one belongs to a person having the Lymphatic and the other the Nervous temperament, there will be a great difference in the way their faculties operate.

It should be remembered that in speaking of these temperaments, the kind of constitution is referred to and not the disposition. A man may have all the marks of the Sanguine temperament and yet be inclined to look on the dark side of things. The Bilious temperament does not mean that a person having it is subject to bilious attacks; nor does the Nervous temperament make one nervous and excitable, although he may be either or both.

CHAPTER XI

THE NEW CLASSIFICATION

THE Fowlers and other later phrenologists, while admitting the value of the classification of the Temperaments given in the last chapter, objected to it because at least two of these—the Lymphatic and the Nervous—were the result of unhealthy conditions in the body. Although they thought it necessary to take these conditions into account, they preferred to base their examinations on what they believed to be a simpler and more reliable system. This was founded on the three systems of organs to be found in the human body and each of the higher order of animals. These are: the Motive or Mechanical system; the Vital or Nutritive system; and the Mental or Nervous system. On this natural basis rests their list of the Temperaments, which they named:

1. *The Motive Temperament.*
2. *The Vital Temperament.*
3. *The Mental Temperament.*

Each of these is determined by the ruling power of the class of organs from which it is named.

The first, or mechanical system, is made up of the framework of bone and muscles, united by fibres or tendons, which act like ropes attached to levers, giving the ability to move and act. It corresponds to the Bilious Temperament of the old list.

In the second, or Vital Temperament, the organs rule which give animal strength, energy, and endurance. These include the lungs, heart, stomach, and spleen, whose duty is to make from the food and distribute to all parts of the system the nourishment necessary for health and strength, and to take up and get rid of all waste material. This corresponds, in the old class, to the Sanguine and Lymphatic Temperaments combined.

The third, or Mental Temperament, is marked by the controlling power of the brain and nerves. The brain may be likened to the chief despatcher's office of a railroad, and the nerves to the telegraph lines which run from the office to all parts of the road. Over some of these lines comes the information from the outside world; these correspond to the nerves of feeling or sensation. Out on other lines go the orders which start into mo-

tion the men and machinery required for the successful running of the road; these may be compared to the nerves of motion, which employ the
bones and muscles to bring about a desired result.
And just as the successful running of a railroad
depends largely upon the clearness with which
the information is received at the despatcher's
office, and the sureness with which orders are
carried out, so the success of a man depends upon
the clearness with which his brain, through the
nerves of sensation, receives outside impressions,
and the accuracy and rapidity with which those
of motion respond to his will.

As the brain is the instrument through which
the mind thus acts, and controls as well all nerves
and muscles throughout the entire body, the Mental is the most important of all the temperaments,
but it does not make up the whole of human nature. A combination of all three, working together
in harmony, is necessary to make the perfect man.
But this is rarely found.

Sometimes the Motive Temperament is stronger
than the others; sometimes the Vital; sometimes
the Mental. Yet there is usually more or less of
each temperament in every individual. By studying the person—his form, his features, his manner,

the color of his skin and hair, the temperament that rules can be readily learned, and, though perhaps not quite so readily, the proportions with which it is mixed with the others.

We will now consider the three temperaments separately, and afterward, as they are combined and graded in various ways.

CHAPTER XII

THE TEMPERAMENTS DESCRIBED

LARGE bones, usually long rather than broad, and sharp angular outlines denote

THE MOTIVE TEMPERAMENT

While the muscles are only fairly full, they are firm, dense, and of great strength. The whole body is strong, wiry, and built for great endurance. A long face with high cheek bones, large front teeth, rather long neck, broad shoulders, and a chest showing moderate fulness, are other signs of this temperament. Strongly marked features, with an expression sometimes harsh and stern, are accompanied by a complexion and eyes that are usually dark—though not always—and dark, strong, abundant hair. Leaders in active life who love power and conquest, often going through difficulties that would discourage less strong men to attain their ends, and showing a reckless disregard of their own physical welfare or that of their followers, have these qualities to a great degree.

Phrenologically, their organs of Firmness, Combativeness, and Destructiveness, together with those of perception—Individuality, Form, Size, Weight, etc.—are large or full, making them self-reliant, persevering, ambitious and commanding, constant in love and friendship. They are positive in manner, strong and emphatic in language, and talk directly to the point.

The temperament of Abraham Lincoln was Motive, combined with the Mental. (See Fig. 41.) His height was six feet four inches; he had long, bony arms and legs; a long, strong neck; and his lanky figure throughout was made up of hard muscles covered by firm flesh, but little fat. The study of law and its practice increased his Mental Temperament, which showed itself in his keenness of mind, his wit and humor. The strength of his style in speaking and writing, and the simplicity and earnestness of his sentences, were the result of a Mental Temperament controlled by the Motive. The smoothness and plumpness of the Vital Temperament was in him almost wholly lacking.

The Motive Temperament when too largely developed results in mere animal strength, with little intelligence. The signs are a small head, lacking in the upper, or region of the crown, and broad at

FIG. 41.   ABRAHAM LINCOLN, Motive-Mental Temperament

the base; a neck that is short and thick; broad shoulders; expanded chest, and large, thick muscles visible through the skin; in short, the body of a prize-fighter, remarkable for brute force and little else.

THE VITAL TEMPERAMENT

The marks of this temperament are: a broad, thick trunk, in which the vital organs are located, a well developed stomach, plump and tapering limbs, and relatively small hands and feet. The head and face tend to roundness, the neck is short and thick, and the shoulders broad. The eyes and hair are light, and the complexion usually red or pink; while the expression of the face is mild and agreeable, often mirthful.

Persons of this temperament are active, both in mind and body. They love fresh air and exercise, as well as lively conversation and exciting debate, but are in general, says Fowler, "less inclined to close study or hard work than those in whom the Motive Temperament takes the lead. They are ardent, impulsive, versatile, and sometimes fickle; and possess more diligence than perseverance, and more brilliancy than depth. They are frequently passionate and violent, but are as easily calmed as excited, and are cheerful, amiable,

FIG. 42. PRESIDENT TAFT, Vital-Mental Temperament

and genial in general disposition. Being fond of jovial companions and good living, they are more liable than others to become users of stimulants to an excessive degree, as well as to overeating, and should be on their guard against this danger and curb their appetites with a strong will."

In such persons the animal propensities are usually large—especially Amativeness, Alimentiveness, and Acquisitiveness. Hope, Benevolence, and Mirthfulness are also large or full.

President Taft is a good illustration of the Vital Temperament (Fig. 42). In him the great size of the chest and stomach, the full face, the stout limbs and plump hands, and the well-nourished appearance of the entire system, show a free circulation of rich, red blood, and a healthy condition of the organs of digestion and nutrition. In connection with his fine vital power, the Mental Temperament is shown by his large head, which gives him the fine intelligence and ability to estimate the value of men and issues, which have placed him in the President's chair.

A sluggish action of the organs of circulation, and those devoted to digestion and secretion, produce the unhealthy condition called by the older phrenologists the Lymphatic Temperament, resulting in slowness of action, both mental and physical, laziness and indifference.

THE MENTAL TEMPERAMENT

depending as it does upon the rule of the brain and nerves, gives a head relatively large as compared with the body, which is usually slight. Other signs are an oval or pear-shaped face; high, pale forehead, broad at the top; delicately formed features; expressive countenance; skin of fine texture; fine, soft hair; and a soft, high-keyed voice. While often well formed and graceful, the figure is seldom striking or commanding.

The possessor of this temperament is naturally refined and sensitive; he loves the beautiful, both in art and nature; his thoughts are quick, his senses keen, his imagination vivid and lively, and his moral sentiments active and influential. The animal organs, which lie at the lower part of the head, are usually small as compared with Causality, Comparison, Ideality, Spirituality, and Veneration, which lie behind the upper portion of the forehead and in the region of the crown. This temperament prevails among scholars everywhere.

The picture of Edgar Allen Poe shows an unusually active Mental Temperament (Fig. 43).

FIG. 43. EDGAR ALLEN POE, Mental Temperament

In form he was slight, slender, and delicately formed. His brain was uncommonly large for the size of his face and body, and his features were sharply outlined. His head was wide in its upper part where reason has its seat, and across the temples in the region of Ideality, Constructiveness, and Sublimity. His hair was dark and fine, and both his skull and scalp were thin. His eyes were full and dark, and held a look of noticeable sadness, corresponding with the events of his troubled and varied career.

The undue or unhealthy development of this temperament—resulting from too early and irregular growth of the brain, and built up by an indoor occupation, the excessive use of tea, coffee, tobacco, and other stimulants—brings about a condition corresponding to the Nervous Temperament of the old classification. The signs are described under that head.

Judging the Temperaments

Knowing what to look for as indications of temperament, the student will find little difficulty in arriving at correct conclusions in those cases where the Motive, the Vital, or the Mental plainly governs.

FIG. 44. HON. RICHARD C. KERENS OF MISSOURI,
A Well-Balanced Temperament.

With the living subject before him, he will begin by considering his size and general appearance, as compared with the average development of the sex, race, and nation to which the individual belongs. He will next ask himself these questions:

Are the organs which digest and derive nourishment from the food large and active, as indicated by firm, solid flesh and a healthy color?

Is the lung power and circulation good or bad, as shown by the size of the chest and the strength and steadiness, or otherwise, of the pulse?

Does the size of the head correspond well with the size of the body, or does either one of these seem out of proportion?

Is the person slow or quick in his movements?

Does he seem to be cold and indifferent, or sensitive to impressions, and easily influenced?

The manner in which these questions can be answered will aid the student to arrive at a correct judgment regarding the constitutional make-up of the individual under examination. He should bear in mind all that has been said in previous chapters about the signs of the different temperaments, and ask himself in what degree do these show themselves in the case before him. Is there enough of the Vital Temperament to give all the

FIG. 45. TERESA CARREÑO. Motive-Vital Temperament

energy which could be used to advantage, enough of the Motive to give that energy, power and force in the work of life, and enough of the Mental to direct that power wisely?

In a perfect man it is necessary that all the powers of brain and body work together in harmony. But the perfect man is rare, and even among the masses of the crowded city, it is hard to find a temperament that is at once strong and well balanced. Often one phase of individual temperament will be found strong, while other phases are weak.

Another thing should be borne in mind. While harmony of temperament is very desirable, this balance may exist without strength. That is, all the qualities that go to make up that balance may themselves be weak, as in a man with a small head and low type of development throughout. Another may have a large head, with splendid mental development, and yet, because he lacks in Vital and Motive power, his actual ability to use his brains to the best advantage may be small.

The best temperament is the one in which the signs of all three are so balanced and strong that even an expert would find it difficult to say which is the most powerful. A good balance of tempera-

FIG. 46. MME. LOUISE HOMER, Vital-Motive Temperament

ments is shown in Fig. 44. The height and width of the forehead denotes an ample Mental Temperament, made vigorous by a well developed Vital—as shown by the smoothness and fulness of the face—and given the power to labor by the strength of the Motive, indicated by the well-proportioned neck and shoulders.

In Fig. 45, a combination of the Motive-Vital seems to rule. A forehead of only moderate development is combined with a face rather long, and well outlined features, both signs of the Motive. The expression is mild and pleasant and the shoulders and chest broad, which are marks of the Vital Temperament.

In Fig. 46, on the other hand, the round face, the short neck, and the broad shoulders and chest show good vital quality. This is combined with fair Motive, as indicated by the dark, abundant hair, the large nose, the width of the side-head above the ears, and the lower part of the forehead, as compared with that of the upper forehead.

In conclusion, it may be said that an understanding of the science of Physiognomy is of great help to the phrenologist. So true is this that many books on Phrenology include the signs of character revealed by the shape of the nose, the ears, the eyes, the mouth, and the chin. In this book the author has devoted himself wholly to the presentation of Phrenology alone, because of its larger importance, and also because Physiognomy has been treated in a complete and interesting manner by Miss Leila Lomax in another volume of this series.

FINIS

Breinigsville, PA USA
09 January 2010
230481BV00001B/68/A